THE HUNTING PIONEERS, 1720–1840
Ultimate Backwoodsmen
on the Early American Frontier

Robert John Holden
With Donna Jean Holden

Robert John Holden
Donna Jean Holden

Heritage Books, Inc.

Published 2000 by

HERITAGE BOOKS, INC.
1540E Pointer Ridge Place, Bowie, Maryland 20716
1-800-398-7709
www.heritagebooks.com

ISBN 0-7884-1526-3

A Complete Catalog Listing Hundreds of Titles
On History, Genealogy, and Americana
Available Free Upon Request

To our parents and our son,
with love and thanks

And to all who
appreciate the wilderness

CONTENTS

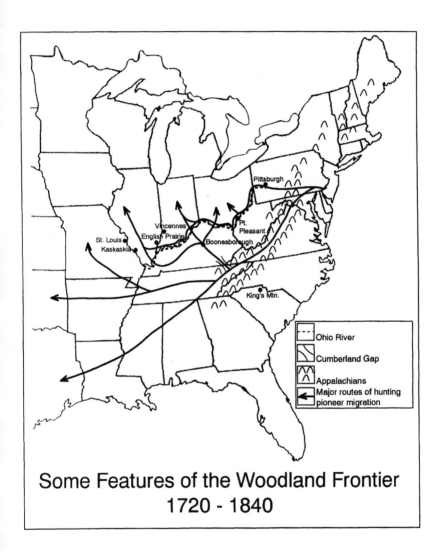

Pittsburgh

Vincennes
English Prairie
St. Louis
Kaskaskia
Boonesborough
Pt. Pleasant

King's Mtn.

Ohio River

Cumberland Gap

Appalachians

Major routes of hunting
pioneer migration

Some Features of the Woodland Frontier
1720 - 1840

INTRODUCTION

This book is about the hunting pioneer families in the early American wilderness. These hunting pioneers in the vast forests of interior America were a truly distinct type, the likes of which the world never had seen before and never would see again. A dynamic force from the early 1700s to the mid-1800s, they led the frontier advance from the western backcountry of Pennsylvania, Maryland, Virginia, the Carolinas, and Georgia, all the way to the edge of the treeless Great Plains. These denizens of the backwoods reveled in their freedom and independence. They were lured on by a craving for forested wilderness, the only environment in which their lifestyle could exist. Following behind and sometimes overtaking the *hunting* pioneers were the much more numerous *farming* pioneers who methodically destroyed the wilderness with their axes and plows.

The hunting pioneers, often illiterate, left virtually no written records. Fortunately for posterity, however, detailed and expressive eyewitness accounts of these wilderness families were written by a large number of travelers who journeyed through the vast wooded domain of the hunting pioneers from the 1720s to the 1840s. Most of the wayfarers formed strong opinions about the colorful backwoods inhabitants, using such contradictory terms as friendly, slothful, intelligent, indolent, honest, slovenly, kind, drunken, daring, rough, hardy, unsociable, trustworthy, fearless, ignorant, and vigilant. The narratives produced by the American and foreign observers originated as books, journals, and letters. The vivid descriptions provide perceptive and in-depth portraits of these unique frontier people and their relationship to the vast, all-encompassing, forest wilderness which surrounded them. Although often used by historians, these accounts had not been analyzed specifically and systematically for the great insight they provide into the lives of the hunting pioneers. Among the travelers and sojourners who observed the hunting pioneers and their wilderness environment were: John James Audubon (American), Francis Baily (English), Morris Birkbeck (English), William Newnham Blane (English), John Brandmueller (Swiss), William Byrd (American), Georges Henri Victor Collot (French), J. Hector St. John de Crevecoeur (French), Fortescue Cuming (English), Eliza W. Farnham (American), William Faux (English), Henry Bradshaw Fearon (English), John Filson (American), Gershom Flagg (American), James Flint (Scotch), Timothy Flint (American), George Flower (English), Elias Pym Fordham (English), Friedrich Gerstacker (German), Thaddeus Mason Harris (American), A. D. Jones (American), Hugh McCulloch (American), Francois Andre Michaux (French), William Oliver (English), John Mason Peck (American), Benjamin Rush (American), Leonhard Schnell (German), Johann David Schoepf (German), Henry Rowe Schoolcraft (American), Charles Woodmason (English), and John Stillman Wright (American).

It definitely is important to note that these middle- and upper-class travelers, both foreign and native to these shores, often brought their prejudices and preconceived ideas with them as they journeyed west. The fact that they came from a much higher social strata than the people they were describing inevitably would color their observations. For virtually all of these writers, the hunting pioneer family was a unique and startling phenomenon, in sharp contrast to the people with whom they normally associated. In some cases, the difference in backgrounds between the observer and the observed probably caused the former to be excessively critical. In other instances, the Romantic literary influence then in vogue may have resulted in an overly favorable appraisal. Still, some writers seemed able to present a balanced viewpoint. This present study does not attempt to analyze the individual biases of these authors. A general conclusion regarding the character of the hunting pioneers based on the totality of the material examined is provided in the **Summary** of this book.

The eyewitness accounts provide the only really reliable information on the hunting pioneers. Collectors of early frontier reminiscences and documents, such as Lyman Copeland Draper and Reverend John Dabney Shane, gathered a wealth of information on many subjects. Unfortunately, their material does not differentiate specifically and in great detail between hunting pioneers and farming pioneers, as do the travelers' accounts which furnish the documentation for this study.

Finally, a word on Daniel Boone, whose very fame makes mandatory his appearance from time to time in these pages. Boone owes his prominent place in American history and folklore to a combination of factors, including his adventurous exploits in the backwoods and an early widely read book on frontier Kentucky which contained his purported memoirs. He thus became in his own lifetime the most noted individual who had spent at least a portion of his life as a hunting pioneer. Unlike the majority of that type, however, Boone at times in his later years took up other varied occupations. This present book limits its sporadic mention of Boone to his place in the overall history of the hunting pioneers. It is certain from all indications that he shared with this particular group most of the basic characteristics which were delineated by travelers.

Chapter 1, **An Overview**, provides an introductory look at the hunting pioneer families from the beginning to the end of their era. Several eyewitness accounts are utilized. Examining the significance of the hunting pioneers' role in American frontier history, the chapter details the similarities and differences among the hunting pioneers and their two greatest nemeses: the Indians and the farming pioneers.

Chapter 2, **The Era Begins**, briefly goes back to ancient times tracing mankind's relationship with the wilderness. It then explores both the Old World and New World backgrounds of the people who would become the hunting pioneers. The initial advance of this distinctive and evolving frontier people is followed as they move gradually westward through the backcountry of Pennsylvania, Maryland, Virginia, the Carolinas, and Georgia, and then finally across the Appalachian Mountain barrier into portions of Kentucky and Tennessee. Several eyewitness accounts of the hunting pioneer families are provided.

Chapter 3, **Wilderness Warfare**, surveys the background of the Indian wars in the forests of North America before focusing on the strategies and tactics of the hunting pioneers and the farming pioneers in their combined fight against the Native Americans. Eleven armed clashes during the Revolutionary War era are covered in some depth. These battles, including several in which the British and Loyalists played an important role, illustrate the no-holds-barred nature of this frontier warfare. The actions occurred during a period in which the Indians were a powerful presence and while the pioneers were fighting without significant aid from regular troops. Because travelers were not present during this period of intense conflict to record their impressions of the hunting pioneers, this is the only chapter without that specific type of eyewitness material.

Chapter 4, **The Ohio River Valley**, provides a large number of eyewitness descriptions illustrating how the lifestyle of the hunting pioneers developed as these people progressed through present-day West Virginia, Kentucky, Ohio, and

Indiana following the Revolutionary War. The direct and growing threat of the farming pioneers to that way of life is examined. Particular emphasis is given to those hunting pioneers living near the Ohio River, where they readily were observed by early travelers moving through the region. Chapter 5, **The Illinois Country**, tells in great detail through many eyewitness accounts how the hunting pioneers perfected their lifestyle in the Illinois country, particularly during the period following the War of 1812. Their interaction with the Indians and the farming pioneers is explored. Through a combination of circumstances, it was in this time and place that the greatest number of travelers recorded their impressions of these colorful people. Several of the wayfarers lingered for a significant time in the area and thus were able to appraise fully these backwoods inhabitants, sometimes with radically differing conclusions.

Chapter 6, **The South and Across the Mississippi**, continues the eyewitness accounts, following the hunting pioneers into the wilds of what is now Tennessee, Alabama, and Mississippi. Then the saga of these frontier people proceeds as they cross the Mississippi River and move throughout the forests of present-day Missouri, Arkansas, eastern Oklahoma, Louisiana, and eastern Texas, all the way to the edge of the Great Plains. There, the era in which the hunting pioneer families advanced ever onward into the deep woods comes to an end.

The **Summary** provides an overall portrait of the hunting pioneers based on the eyewitness descriptions in the earlier chapters. The role of these unique people in the history of the American frontier is summarized. The hunting pioneers' attitude toward the wilds is compared with the thoughts expressed by those giants of the modern wilderness movement, Henry David Thoreau and John Muir. Currently, as efforts are underway in the United States to preserve additional areas of wilderness, the tremendous attraction which life in the wilds held for the hunting pioneers is particularly relevant. Their experiences provide the present generation with one of the most illuminating case studies of the interaction of people and wilderness.

1

AN OVERVIEW

The hunting pioneer families, the most unique and colorful group on the American woodland frontier, were the ultimate wilderness archetypes. Simplifying existence down to the bare necessities, they single-mindedly pursued their goal of living in the backwoods. Here is life as it really was two centuries ago in the vast forests extending from the backcountry of Pennsylvania, Maryland, Virginia, the Carolinas, and Georgia, all the way to the eastern edge of the Great Plains. In order to recreate the scene vividly, while achieving the greatest accuracy, a multitude of detailed eyewitness accounts by travelers on the frontier are utilized.

The hunting pioneers, variously referred to by contemporary observers as hunters, hunter-farmers, backwoodsmen, forest men, first inhabitants, back settlers, or squatters, continually plunged into new wilds, savoring the freedom those wilds offered. On the cutting edge of the frontier and among the first to confront the Indians in their own domain, the *hunting* pioneers had a perception of the wilderness which was totally different from that of the *farming* pioneers who far outnumbered them. The former continually sought out remote lands where the wild animals roamed; the latter followed behind and systematically destroyed that wilderness on which the game depended, in order to plant extensive crops and create pasturage for their livestock. This encroachment by the farming pioneers forced the hunting pioneers to move on, and the process was repeated again and again until finally the vast woodlands were gone. Hated by the Indians, often scorned by their fellow countrymen, later idealized by a public who did not recognize fully their distinctiveness, the hunting pioneers were a vital factor in the westward expansion of the nation.

The origin of the American hunting pioneers can be traced to the mid-1600s and the deep forests along the Delaware River in what is now western New Jersey, eastern Pennsylvania, and northern Delaware. The Swede-Finn inhabitants of the short-lived colony of New Sweden had arrived at that location in the New World with a long history of living in a wooded wilderness. As their deep woods lifestyle in their new homeland evolved, they were influenced greatly by the local Indians. Over the years, these Swede-Finns were joined by some English and Germans also attracted to life in those eastern forests. It was not until the arrival of successive waves of Scotch-Irish immigrants in Pennsylvania during the early decades of the 1700s, however, that the hunting pioneer ethos would be adopted by a sufficient number of people to make it a dynamic force in a suddenly accelerated westward expansion, first to the Appalachian Mountains and then far beyond. Throughout this period from 1720 to 1840, the combined Swede-Finn and Scotch-Irish influences would dominate both the mind-set and the lifestyle of the hunting pioneers.[1]

In his book, *Travels in the Confederation, 1783-1784*, Johann David Schoepf gives the following description of the hunting pioneers on the western frontier of Pennsylvania: "These hunters or 'backwoodsmen' live very much like Indians and acquire similar ways of thinking. They shun everything which appears to demand of them law and order, dread anything which breathes constraint." Schoepf states, nonetheless, that these people are not lawbreakers. "Their object is merely wild, altogether natural freedom, and hunting is what pleases them. An insignificant cabin of unhewn logs; corn and a little wheat, a few cows and pigs, this is all their riches, but they need no more. They get game from the woods; skins bring them in whiskey and clothes, which they do not care for of a costly sort. Their habitual costume is a 'rifle-shirt,' or shirt of fringed linen; instead of stockings they wear Indian leggings; their shoes they make themselves for the most part." Schoepf explains that when going on extended hunting trips these men take only salt and cornmeal to eat; for the rest of their food they rely on the wild game they kill. "Thus they pass 10 to 20 days in the woods; wander far around; shoot whatever appears; take only the skins, the tongues, and some venison back with them on their horses to their cabins, where the meat is smoked and dried; the rest is left lying in the woods. They look upon the wilderness as their home, and the wild life as their possession; and so by this wandering, uncertain way of life, of which they are vastly fond, they become indifferent to all social ties, and do not like many neighbors about them, who by scaring off the game are a nuisance besides." These hunting pioneers often bring back from their hunts a great quantity of furs, which are of considerable value in trade. "Uncompanionable and truculent as this sort of men appear to be, and however they seem half-savage and, by their manner of life, proof against the finer feelings, one is quite safe among them and well treated; they have their own way of being courteous and agreeable which not everybody would take to be what it is. Their little housekeeping is, for their situation, neat; and their wives and children are content in their solitudes where for the most part they spend the time in idleness."[2]

Only by continually keeping in mind the wilds in which they existed can we today approach a full understanding of the essential nature of the hunting pioneers, a people whom their contemporaries considered the real frontiersmen and the ultimate backwoodsmen. When the Europeans first arrived in the New World, more than four-fifths of the forested land in what is now the United States was east of the Great Plains; the remainder was in the far West from the Rocky Mountains to the Pacific Coast. Those great forests in the eastern half of the continent contained natural prairies and clearings, some the result of periodic wildfires. In addition, the Native Americans used fire to create open areas of grass in their forest hunting grounds. These spaces provided superior browsing conditions which, in conjunction with the protective woods, attracted and sustained large game populations. Despite these natural and man-made modifications, there remained an immense expanse of wooded wilderness east of the Great Plains.[3]

Traveling in the region between the Appalachian Mountains and the Mississippi River in the second decade of the 1800s, Elias Pym Fordham wrote, "You will never have a correct idea of what a wilderness is till you come to visit me. It is no more like a great wood, than a battle is like a review." He notes that regardless of the area's size as indicated by charts or maps, "the traveller and hunter find impediments," which make it seem larger.[4]

"To be at an unknown distance from the dwellings of man; to have pathless forests of trees around you; and intervening rivers, across which you must swim on your horse or on a raft, whatever be the temperature of the water or the air;—the whispering breeze among the leaves, the spring of the deer, or the flap of the Eagle's wing are the only sounds you hear during the day; and then to lie at night in a blanket, with your feet to a fire, your rifle hugged in your arms, listening to the howling wolves, and starting at the shriek of the terrible panther: This is to be in a Wilderness alone."[5]

Despite Fordham's phrase "pathless forests," in reality many trails ran through these woods as a result of use through the ages by both the wild animals and the Indians. Some of the widest and deepest trails had been made by buffalo herds which ranged through the woods both east and west of the Mississippi River, far from the Great Plains haunts usually associated with the buffalo. In addition, easy access through the interior forests from the Appalachian Mountains to the Great Plains was provided by many waterways, including the Ohio, Muskingham, Kanawha, Scioto, Miami, Kentucky, Wabash, Cumberland, Tennessee, Mississippi, Missouri, Arkansas, and Red rivers. The forest was largely deciduous and varied from thickly situated trees to those more widely spaced. In many places, the great overhead canopy kept out sunlight and prevented brush from taking over the forest floor.[6]

Roderick Nash explains in *Wilderness and the American Mind* that most Europeans arriving in America found the wilderness particularly forbidding for two reasons. First, on a physical level, the wilds posed a strong obstacle to basic survival. Wilderness was incompatible with any extensive cultivation of crops, and most pioneers depended primarily on agriculture to survive. Thus, they promptly started destroying the wilds in order to create the necessary open space on which to grow food and graze livestock. Second, on a psychological level, wilderness had a long Old World tradition as a dark, chaotic, and ominous wasteland. Civilizing the New World would mean removing the darkness, chaos, and menace of the wilderness condition.[7]

Those particular people who became the hunting pioneers had a far different outlook on wilderness; they were drawn onward by the very wildness of that land. There was, of course, no scale measuring by degrees from hunting pioneer to farming pioneer. Nevertheless, at either end of the spectrum there certainly was an obvious and definite distinction. Hunting pioneer families depended primarily on hunting for food, raised small patch crops only as a supplement to their diet, and let any livestock they possessed run loose in the woods. They normally had little or no desire to own land, usually built only crude dwellings, spent a considerable portion of their time at leisure, and were ready to move on to new wilderness as soon as the increasing population and their own hunting depleted the wild game. Farming pioneer families, by contrast, depended primarily on crops and domestic animals for food, hunted game only as a supplement to their diet, and closely tended or fenced in their livestock. They usually desired to own land, constructed somewhat substantial dwellings and even stables or barns, spent most of their time working, and were less likely to move frequently.

A third group, which combined elements of both the hunting pioneers and the farming pioneers, were the herders and drovers. Often taking advantage of the animals which had run wild and multiplied since early colonial days, these frontier people accumulated substantial herds of cattle or pigs which they loosely tended in the backcountry. The herders and drovers resembled the farming pioneers in their greater reliance on livestock rather than wild game, but they matched the hunting pioneers in their disdain for farming. The herders and drovers were most prevalent in the South; they will be discussed briefly when that specific region is considered.

In his landmark 1893 paper, "The Significance of the Frontier in American History," Frederick Jackson Turner achieved prominence among historians with the theory that the wilderness conditions on the westward-advancing frontier were a major factor in the evolution of a distinctly American character. Turner's thesis has been the subject of unending controversy for generations of historians. His detractors fault him for not taking into proper account the part played by economics, urbanization, and industrialization, or the role of women, African Americans, and Native Americans. Nevertheless, Turner's emphasis on the influence of the wilderness environment in American history certainly applies to this study of the hunting pioneers.[8]

The people who developed into hunting pioneers were influenced greatly by the Native Americans. Again and again, contemporary observers would comment on the similarity of their wilderness lifestyles. In tribal society, skills as a hunter and warrior were viewed as the highest attainments. A premium was placed on courage, hardiness, individualism, and personal freedom. All of these qualities the hunting pioneers would come to embrace wholeheartedly.[9]

The Indians subsisted on a combination of agriculture and hunting. Corn, beans, pumpkins, and squash were the principal crops; deer and bear were the favored game. The women's and older children's chores included planting, harvesting, collecting wild food from the forest, and preparing meals. They also gathered firewood, carried water, tanned hides, made clothing, wove baskets, and cared for the younger children. The Indian men hunted, fished, cleared the land, built the dwellings, and protected their families.[10]

The hunting pioneers adopted into their diet some of the same plants the Indians used, particularly corn, and showed the same preferences in wild game. The women and children did most of the work involved in what limited crops were raised, gathered wild food in the woods, and did the same daily chores as their Indian counterparts. The firearms of the hunting pioneers may have enabled them to depend more on hunting and less on agriculture than the Indians had been able to do with their bows and arrows in pre-European times. Despite the intermittent clashes between Indians and backwoods people, the sporadic mingling of the races during the more peaceful times soon resulted in an admixture of European and Indian blood in a portion of the backcountry population.

From the earliest beginnings of settlement in the English colonies, there had been a fear that the wilderness would overpower the traditions and customs of some of the colonists. The deep woods offered total freedom from the laws and restraints of society. Thus, there was a concern that individuals detaching themselves from the more civilized colonial environs to enter the wilds would sink into utter barbarism.[11]

Fueling the concern over the impact of wilderness on susceptible individuals was the misconception many Europeans had about Native American life and culture. Despite a large number of eyewitness accounts by early English colonists describing tribal economies having significant and successful agriculture, the Indians often were viewed simply as primitive hunters living in the wilderness. This misperception may be attributable, at least in part, to the fact that the men did little of the agricultural work but spent much of their time hunting in the woods. And those who were primarily hunters, whether Indians or colonials, were considered by most Europeans to be savages and a threat to civilized society (the distinctive "noble savage" concept will be discussed in chapters 3 and 4).[12]

In *How the West Was Lost: The Transformation of Kentucky from Daniel Boone to Henry Clay*, Stephen Aron points out that by the mid-1700s many officials and travelers were viewing with alarm the growing class of backwoods people in the deep forests east of the Appalachian Mountains stretching from Pennsylvania to South Carolina. In the opinion of the onlookers, the major problem with these families, particularly those who were hunting pioneers, was that they appeared to be "white Indians." Little in their way of life was thought to distinguish them from the real Indians. According to the observers, the hunting pioneers' addiction to the pursuit of wild game had caused them to revert to the lowest level of subsistence. It was thought that this unrestrained hunting lifestyle ensured the poverty of their circumstances, the shiftlessness of their habits, and the insolence of their behavior. The type of hunting carried on by these backcountry people was seen in sharp contrast to the gentlemanly pursuit of game for sport.[13]

Robert W. McCluggage, in a journal article entitled "The Pioneer Squatter," points out that the hunting pioneers were considered to be as much or more of a threat to established society as the Indians. These "white Indians" illustrated to their contemporaries just how easy it was in the American wilderness to revert to the simpler hunting life. Even more alarming, the backwoodsman's obvious enjoyment of this life showed how attractive this alternative could be.[14]

J. Hector St. John de Crevecoeur, a Frenchman who settled in America after the French and Indian War, makes note of the hunting pioneers during the late colonial period in his *Letters From An American Farmer*. Arriving "near the great woods, near the last inhabited districts," he found the people beyond the reach of government, a situation which caused discord, drunkenness, idleness, contention, and wretchedness. "There men appear to be no better than carnivorous animals of a superior rank, living on the flesh of wild animals when they can catch them and when they are not able they subsist on grain." Crevecoeur explains that these families "are a kind of forlorn hope," who precede by ten or twelve years the much more respectable people who come after them. During that time some of the hunters will improve, but others will be driven off by civilization and recede into the woods.[15]

The dwellings of the hunting pioneer families ranged

from the temporary lean-to to more substantial log structures. A rough log cabin usually was the height of their housing ambitions. Unlike many of the farming pioneers, they had no intention of staying in one area long enough to make the transition to anything more elaborate. The log cabin, whether crudely built or carefully crafted, has gone down in American folk culture as the quintessential American dwelling.

Dr. Benjamin Rush, the noted physician of the Revolutionary and early National eras, was an extensive traveler and prolific writer. He recorded his observations regarding the hunting pioneers on the western Pennsylvania frontier in a letter written in 1786: "The first settler in the woods is generally a man who has outlived his credit or fortune in the cultivated parts of the state. His time for migrating is in the month of April. His first object is to build a small cabin of rough logs for himself and family. The floor of his cabin is of earth, the roof of split logs; the light is received through the door and, in some instances, through a small window made of greased paper."[16]

Rush relates that the hunting pioneers kill some trees (by cutting a circle around them beneath the bark), prepare the ground, and plant some Indian corn. In September, this crop provides considerable nourishment in the form of roasting ears. "His family is fed during the summer by a small quantity of grain which he carries with him, and by fish and game. His cows and horses feed upon wild grass and the succulent twigs of the woods. . . . As he lives in the neighborhood of Indians, he soon acquires a strong tincture of their manners. His exertions, while they continue, are violent, but they are succeeded by long intervals of rest. His pleasures consist chiefly in fishing and hunting. He loves spirituous liquors, and he eats, drinks and sleeps in dirt and rags in his little cabin."[17]

The hunting pioneers described by Rush live in the area

for two or three years, but they become dissatisfied and uneasy as other people move in around them. "Formerly he fed his family with wild animals, but these, which fly from the face of man, now cease to afford him an easy subsistence, and he is compelled to raise domestic animals for the support of his family." Moving on, the hunting pioneers retreat into the woods, a process which likely will be repeated several times during their lives.[18]

The lifestyle of the hunting pioneers during their major advance through the wilderness from 1720 to 1840 was made possible by the firearms which they carried with them. In this regard, these frontier people were fortunate in three ways. First, by 1700 the flintlock igniting system had replaced entirely the unreliable and impractical matchlock. Second, in 1710 German gunsmiths newly arrived in southeastern Pennsylvania began making firearms with short, rifled barrels following their Old World tradition. These rifles had a longer range and were more accurate than smoothbore firearms, which had been the only type of weapon available in the colonies. Third, by 1720 the main path of migration for successive waves of frontier people would take them through the very region in southeastern Pennsylvania where the new guns were being made. Thus, during the next several decades, the hunting pioneers would become well acquainted with the early German rifle or its later evolutions.[19]

The German gunsmiths in Pennsylvania, in an effort to increase the range and accuracy of their rifles to meet the needs of the frontiersmen in the New World, soon began making rifles with longer barrels; they also gave the weapon a slimmer stock than had been used on the shorter rifles. In this new design, these gunsmiths were duplicating to some extent the look of the long-barreled, smoothbore, English fowling piece which at that time was prevalent in the colonies. By about

1750, this new and improved rifle had evolved essentially into what would be known as the long rifle. Although some frontiersmen would continue to use shorter-barreled rifles or even smoothbores, the long rifle soon became the firearm of choice for most pioneers, particularly the hunting pioneers. With a rifled barrel more than forty inches long, this weapon was highly effective at a distance of 150 yards or more; by comparison, the accuracy of the smoothbore musket quickly diminished beyond fifty yards. Unlike the musket, which often was as large as .75 caliber, most long rifles ranged from .35 to .50 or .60 caliber. The smaller diameter of the long rifle barrel conserved powder and lead, an important consideration when one lived far from supplies or went on extended hunting trips.[20]

The long rifle was the most prized possession of the frontiersman; it was especially valued by the hunting pioneer. Never far from his side, the long rifle was like an extension of the hunting pioneer's personality and seemed to define his very nature. It was essential to the preservation of his life both in hunting and in warfare. This weapon would play a prominent role in the fighting west of the Appalachians during the Revolutionary War, as well as in subsequent conflicts on the woodland frontier. As the years progressed, the makers of the long rifle further refined its design by making the stock progressively slimmer. The butt of the weapon was given a more graceful contour with a slightly downward curve. Hardwood stocks with beautiful graining were complemented by intricate carvings. A large amount of metal ornamentation also was added to the stocks of many of these weapons, particularly in the form of inlays, plates, and patch boxes on the butt. Eventually, the long rifle was being made not only in Pennsylvania, but in several other states as well. The skills of gunmakers varied, as did the quality of the weapons being produced. Although hunting pioneers certainly would have preferred to own the best long rifles, some of them made do with inferior ones. By 1815, this weapon had become known as the Kentucky long rifle because of its close association with the frontiersmen of that region. This firearm still would be in use at the end of the hunting pioneer era in 1840.[21]

Two other essential items used by the hunting pioneers were the ax and the knife. The ax was used for building a rough dwelling, for chopping firewood, and for clearing enough space to allow sunlight into the forest to grow a small crop of corn. The knife was used in hunting and in warfare.

The hunting pioneer families realized that for them freedom and hunting were inextricably intertwined; only hunting would enable them to live in the wilderness beyond the bounds of society with a way of life in which they took great pleasure. Their appreciation of this lifestyle undoubtedly was enhanced by the realization that in the Old World from which they came, such an existence no longer was possible. There, a highly structured society limited many aspects of personal freedom. With the virtual disappearance of significant wild areas in Europe, the pursuit of what game remained had become a sporting pastime increasingly reserved for the upper classes; the lower classes often were forbidden to hunt even on their own lands. Moreover, penalties for game law violations could include summary execution. Yet, here in the great American forest wilderness were large animals useful for their meat and hides, such as deer, bear, buffalo, and elk, which made the hunting privileges of kings and nobles look paltry by comparison. In addition, smaller animals such as beaver and otter could be trapped for their valuable furs.[22]

Animals had been hunted for thousands of years by the Native Americans without serious depletion for these reasons: 1) the limited Indian population; 2) the reliance on bows and arrows; 3) the conservation practices of the Indian hunters who normally killed only what they needed; and 4) a highly elaborate spiritual outlook regarding their natural surroundings, a wilderness world in which animals played a very important and much revered role. The conservation habits among the Indians changed to a significant extent with the advent of the Europeans. In the 1600s, the tribes began killing large numbers of animals in order to exchange the furs and hides for greatly desired European trade goods. Despite this increased hunting and trapping, a multitude of animals still roamed the woods at the arrival of the hunting pioneers.

Deer were by far the most important prey during the entire era of the hunting pioneer families. Venison was a staple of their backwoods diet, and deerskin was used for both clothing and trade purposes. In the course of a lifetime, individual hunters killed hundreds, and sometimes even thousands, of these animals either by stalking in the daytime or by hunting with torches at night. Annually, huge numbers of deerskins were sold to traders by the hunting pioneers. The deerskins were much easier to transport than the bulkier bear, buffalo, and elk hides.

Black bears were also a favorite game animal of hunting pioneers for meat and hides, as well as for the excitement involved in the potentially perilous encounter. Bear fat was highly desired for cooking. The pelts were used for outer winter clothing, blankets, or rugs. Bears usually were hunted with the aid of dogs, which would chase down their prey or "tree" them. In the winter the dogs helped locate the dens. When lean, bears were quick and agile; as they put on weight in preparation for winter, they became slower and more awkward. If cornered, or if protecting cubs, bears suddenly could become ferocious antagonists. Many hunting pioneers were attacked after failing to kill one of these animals with the first shot; the bear's strength, combined with sharp teeth and claws, made such close confrontations extremely dangerous. Buffalo were a popular game animal with the hunting pioneers throughout the eastern woodlands. Buffalo meat was high on their preference list, along with the bone marrow and tallow. The hides made ideal blankets, rugs, tarps, and winter moccasins. Buffalo wool from the head, neck, and shoulders could be woven into cloth. The hides also could be stretched over a wood framework to make crude boats. The buffalos' habit of traveling in herds and gathering in great numbers at salt licks made them easy prey for hunters, and they rapidly were hunted to extinction east of the Great Plains.

Elk also were common in the eastern forests when the hunting pioneers first arrived. They were utilized as food, and their hides made particularly good moccasins and straps. As with the buffalo, elk hides were used to construct boats. Elk tended to travel in large droves and soon were decimated in the domain of the hunting pioneer.

Panthers and wolves were hunted primarily because they were killing the hunting pioneers' limited livestock and competing with them for game. In addition, the backwoodsmen sometimes were able to collect a bounty, particularly in the case of wolves. Panthers usually were pursued with dogs.

Raccoons, squirrels, rabbits, and wild turkeys also were hunted, the first three for their fur as well as for their meat. Normally a rifle of smaller caliber was used. These animals were the first quarry for young boys beginning their hunting careers.

Hunting pioneers usually kept packs of dogs around their cabins. In dangerous times these lean and rangy hounds could give warning of warriors in the dark woods outside the clearing, which might mean the difference between survival and death. During such hazardous periods, however, if the pioneer took his dogs along when hunting, he risked alerting

Indians with their barking. In times of peace, dogs often accompanied hunters in large packs ranging to a dozen or more. They normally were of most value when they were tracking and pursuing an animal which could be treed, thus allowing time for the hunter to catch up. Many hunting dogs met a fatal end fighting a cornered animal, sometimes in defense of their masters. A particularly good hunting dog would be remembered in tales told around the fire long after its death.

The hunting pioneers never gave the same emphasis to trapping as did the French and Indians of the northern Great Lakes region or the later mountain men of the far West. The thinner fur pelts of the animals found in the more temperate forests of the hunting pioneers were not as prime and valuable. In addition, these backwoodsmen probably preferred the thrill of the chase to the more laborious and routine work of setting and tending traps. Nevertheless, some trapping was done.

The season for trapping beaver and otter began as their fur thickened for winter. Beaver were easy to locate due to their dams and lodges. Traps were prepared with bait. Otter were much harder to locate than beaver, although they also lived along the streams. A favorite place for trapping otter was where their slides went down the bank into the water. Bait normally was not used. Both beaver and otter pelts had significant value as trade items.

The clothes of the hunting pioneers reflected the styles then worn among the lower classes in Europe and eastern America, modified by the use of animal hides and locally produced fabrics. In addition, these frontier people were influenced by the apparel of the Indians. For the men and boys, shirts, breeches, and moccasins were made out of animal hides, deerskin being the most frequently used; some of the hunting pioneers adopted the Indian-style breechcloth (or breechclout).

However, hide clothing did have the serious drawbacks of being hot in summer, uncomfortable when wet, and slow to dry. As a result, the hunting pioneers also wore shirts, breeches, and breechcloths made of woven material, usually homemade. Cotton, linen, wool, and a linen and wool combination called linsey-woolsey were fabrics used for clothing. Indian-style leggings, made of either hide or a thick blanket-like material, extended from the ankle to the knee or mid-thigh, providing protection from brush and at least some safeguard against snakebite. Often the hunting pioneers wore a combination of animal skin and cloth clothing.

In cooler weather a hunting jacket (often referred to as a hunting shirt or frock) was worn. It usually was made of woven material or, less frequently, deerskin. This outer garment was cut full to overlap in front and reached down to the middle thigh or knee. A large cape collar normally extended well over the shoulders. The collar, sleeves, and bottom edge of the jacket often were fringed. A wide belt, either leather or woven cloth, went around the jacket. Hats usually were made of felt and had a large brim; fur caps also were worn. In coldest weather, hunting pioneers wore a long and hooded blanket coat modeled after the French capote or wrapped themselves in blankets or fur skins.

The women and girls of hunting pioneer families also wore jackets, dresses, and moccasins of animal skins, as well as clothing created from homemade fabric. Sometimes clothing was made from purchased cloth, or ready-made apparel was obtained. Calico, a patterned cotton cloth, was the trade material seen most frequently. The long cloth dresses, petticoats (skirts), and shifts (smock-like undergarments) were similar to those of the poorer classes elsewhere. However, females in the backwoods concerned themselves foremost with utility and practicality. They often hitched up their dresses or skirts when working and normally went barefoot during warmer weather. Shawls, blanket coats, blankets, or animal furs provided warmth during winter months.

By the time the hunting pioneers were crossing the Appalachian Mountains in the 1760s and 1770s, both their hunting skills and their desire to hunt had reached a zenith. Arthur K. Moore, in *The Frontier Mind: A Cultural Analysis of the Kentucky Frontiersman*, states that although hunting was necessary for survival, the hunting pioneers seemed to derive great pleasure in the mere killing of these animals, as indicated by their wanton destruction of wildlife. He notes that the wastefulness exhibited by the hunters in the Kentucky wilderness presaged the much later destruction of the buffalo herds by hunters far to the west on the Great Plains.[23]

Throughout the years, the hunting pioneers diligently pursued their goal of living in the wilds. During that time, most of them made many successive moves westward. Along the way, some hunting pioneers gradually made the transition to farming pioneers. For those who kept heading into new wilderness, however, each leap onward only confirmed their commitment to what they believed was the best of all lifestyles.

On their trek through the forest, the hunting pioneer families typically brought with them one or two cows for milking and a small number of pigs; a horse or two carried their possessions. Although cattle and sheep had been the primary domesticated animals of the Swede-Finns and Scotch-Irish in the Old World, in America pigs quickly became the predominant livestock among these people and the other hunting pioneers in the backwoods. Running loose in the forests, the hogs thrived, multiplied quickly, and often became so wild they had to be hunted like game. For the hunting pioneers, cattle usually were of secondary importance and sheep were rare.[24]

James Flint's *Letters from America, 1818-1820* gives that Scottish writer's description of the hunting pioneers in the Trans-Appalachian wilderness. Interestingly, it indicates little change in their way of life from the accounts written several decades earlier, except that by this later date at least a portion of these frontiersmen actually were acquiring land legally. "All who have paid attention to the progress of new settlements, agree in stating, that the first possession of the woods in America, was taken by a class of hunters, commonly called backwoodsmen. These, in some instances, purchased the soil from the government, and in others, placed themselves on the public lands without permission. Many of them, indeed, settled new territories before the ground was surveyed, and before public sales commenced." Flint indicates that there had been problems with pre-emption rights which gave purchasing preference to those people already on the land. "The improvements of a backwoodsman are usually confined to building a rude log cabin, clearing and fencing a small piece of ground for raising Indian corn. A horse, a cow, a few hogs, and some poultry, comprise his livestock; and his farther operations are performed with his rifle. The formation of a settlement in his neighborhood is hurtful to the success of his favourite pursuit, and is the signal for his removing into more remote parts of the wilderness. In the case of his owning the land on which he has settled, he is contented to sell it at a low price, and his establishment, though trifling, adds much to the comfort of his successor."[25]

In addition to providing the setting in which the hunting pioneers could perfect their lifestyle, the wilderness also served as a very effective filter from outside interferences and concerns. The personal freedom of the hunting pioneers would exceed even that of the Indians, whose independence necessarily was circumscribed by membership in a communal society. In contrast, the hunting pioneer families, rejecting much of their own society and often living far from their nearest neighbors, knew no such limitations on their freedom. The debate over the form of government to be established after the Revolutionary War seemed of small consequence to those living beyond the bounds of civilization. The growing political partisanship after 1800, likewise, had a minor influence on backwoodsmen, who were too remote to get regular news or take part in the election process. Economic subjects such as depressions, taxes, and tariffs were not a factor where society and government had little or no effect. Even the growing sectionalism and the increasing controversy over the slavery issue in the first half of the nineteenth century had limited impact on families deep in the wilderness. Although people less isolated might choose to ignore many of these issues, they could not achieve the type of physical separation from outside influences as did the hunting pioneers. Only the need for those manufactured goods which they could not produce locally kept the hunting pioneer families from further severing ties with civilization.

Warfare did have immediate and serious repercussions in the wilds. Large-scale conflicts, including the French and Indian War (1755-1763), Pontiac's Rebellion (1763-1765), the American Revolution and its extended aftermath (1775-1794), the War of 1812 (1812-1815), and Black Hawk's War (1832) increased and exacerbated the normal unease and hostility between the Indians and the frontiersmen. These wars also pitted the American pioneers first against the French, and then against the British. On the cutting edge of the frontier advance, the hunting pioneers were in a particularly vulnerable and precarious location. Even so, they were able to thrive and flourish in the relatively peaceful interludes between conflicts.

For the most part, the outside world had little impact on life in the wilds. The hunting pioneers were immersed contentedly in the wilderness, and "no news was good news." Their attraction to the unsettled hunting life was matched only by their antipathy for the settled farming existence. Unlike the farming pioneers, the hunting pioneers were not tied irrevocably to the chores of the season. They lived each day for the day, enjoying their life in the forest. Unbothered by other people's characterization of them as shiftless, lazy, and lacking in ambition, they reveled in the freedom and simplified lifestyle which were theirs.

The predominant religious groups on the frontier were the Presbyterians, Baptists, and Methodists, but several smaller sects also flourished. Even though the isolation of the hunting pioneers placed them beyond the normal reaches of organized religion, many of them still would have been familiar with the basic precepts of the Bible. Some were visited occasionally by itinerant or circuit-riding preachers. Nevertheless, it seems a portion of the hunting pioneers remained heedless of any religion.

In "The Significance of the Frontier in American History," Frederick Jackson Turner quoted a passage from John Mason Peck's *New Guide to the West*, published in Boston in 1837, which contained a description of the hunting pioneers near the end of their era. Peck, a Baptist minister, had lived and traveled for many years west of the Appalachian Mountains, a fact which may have given his observations particular weight in Turner's view. "Generally in all the western settlements, three classes, like the waves of the ocean, have rolled one after the other. First comes the pioneer, who depends for the susbsistence of his family chiefly upon the natural growth of vegetation, called the 'range,' and the proceeds of hunting." Trees are girdled with a deep notch to kill them, and a crop of corn is planted, along with a garden of cabbage, cucumbers, beans, and potatoes. "It is quite immaterial whether he ever becomes the owner of the soil. He is the occupant for the time being, pays no rent, and feels as independent as the 'lord of the manor.' With a horse, cow, and one or two breeders of swine, he strikes into the woods with his family, and becomes the founder of a new county, or perhaps state. He builds his cabin, gathers around him a few other families of similar tastes and habits, and occupies till the range is somewhat subdued, hunting a little precarious, or, which is more frequently the case, till neighbors crowd around, roads, bridges, and fields annoy him, and he lacks elbow room." Then, to use the hunting pioneer's own words, he "breaks for the high timber," to begin all over again.[26]

Peck relates that the next immigrants purchase land, clear more fields for crops, and build substantial dwellings. They also construct mills, schoolhouses, and courthouses. The third group consists of men of capital and enterprise who complete the civilizing process, as the small village grows into a town or city with churches and colleges.[27]

Inevitably, the way of life of the hunting pioneers in the wilds was doomed to the same fate as that of the Native Americans. Ironically, these backwoodsmen served as the agents of their own downfall in two ways, both of which made it easier for the farming pioneers to press closely on their heels. First, by always pushing into the wilderness, the hunting pioneers kept up pressure on the Indians by their presence and by their depletion of the wild game. Second, through periodic cooperation with the much more numerous farming pioneers, they helped to defeat the tribes (although following the Revolutionary War much of the decisive fighting was done by the newly formed United States Army with the frontiersmen usually in a supporting role).

For a time, with each forward move, the hunting pioneer families were able to immerse themselves in a type of wilderness environment which harkened back to the distant dawn of mankind. Moving ever westward, by the 1840s the hunting pioneers had reached the Great Plains and had run out of the woodlands with which they were familiar. In the process, they had been on the forward wave of the frontier, moving through the forested wilds of what is now western Pennsylvania, western Maryland, western Virginia, western North Carolina, western South Carolina, northwestern Georgia, West Virginia, Kentucky, Ohio, Indiana, Illinois, Tennessee, Alabama, Mississippi, Missouri, Arkansas, eastern Oklahoma, Louisiana, and eastern Texas.

The hunting pioneer families were able to maintain their frontier lifestyle for more than a century in these ways: 1) by repeatedly moving on to the next wooded wilderness where there was ready access to game, fuel, and building materials; 2) by taking along a horse or two, a few hogs, and usually at least one cow; 3) by establishing a temporary camp, often consisting of a lean-to, or sometimes simply a rock overhang; 4) by building a rough cabin; 5) by killing or cutting down enough trees in the forest to allow in sunlight for a small crop; 6) by relying on the hunt for the major portion of their food; 7) by utilizing hides and furs for their own needs and for trading; and 8) by not lingering long in an area after the arrival of the first farming pioneers.

In *Westward Expansion: A History of the American Frontier*, Ray Allen Billington describes the hunting pioneers' ultimate nemeses, the farming pioneers, as people who did not compromise with nature; they chopped down the forests and plowed the prairies. Although many farming pioneers also moved frequently with the shifting frontier, their main goal was to civilize nature as had been done behind them. This was the specter which haunted the hunting pioneers. In their worst nightmares, they were pursued by the farming pioneers with their axes and plows.[28]

Unfortunately, an element missing in many of the travelers' descriptions of the hunting pioneer families is a real sense of how the women felt about their lives deep in the forest wilderness far from civilization. It was the men who were able to maximize the benefits of this lifestyle through hunting and roaming, while the women were restricted to the environs of the cabin by child rearing and the daily chores. Those travelers who do describe the hunting pioneer women in some detail usually indicate that they were at least outwardly content with their lives in the deep woods. In fact, some of the women appear no less caught up in this backwoods way of life than were the men. Whatever their inner feelings, the hunting pioneer women exhibited the same incredible courage and hardiness as the men, while these families inexorably swept westward through the wilderness.[29]

2

THE ERA BEGINS

In order to put the American hunting pioneers in the proper perspective, it is necessary to go back briefly to the beginning of mankind when the whole world was wilderness. Humans, initially wandering gatherers of plants, eventually became hunters as well. As indicated by ancient cave art, these early people probably thought of themselves as an integral part of the natural world. Wilderness was everywhere; it was all they knew. Life continued in this manner for untold millenia. Then, sometime after 10,000 B.C., momentous changes began to occur in certain areas of the world. By 6,000 B.C., two new and distinctly different ways of living had appeared in the Fertile Crescent of the Middle East. Some people now were herding animals which once had been hunted; other people were cultivating plants which once had been gathered. Those who primarily had hunted may have become herders to supplement their pursuit of game. Those who mainly had gathered may have become cultivators of crops. The first way of life involved continuing to rove; the second eventually led to permanent agricultural settlements. As these settlements grew, an obvious line developed between civilization and wilderness. Soon, these farming people viewed the now unfamiliar wilds with apprehension. This fear was compounded by the fact that from the wilderness nomadic hunters and herders periodically descended as raiders and conquerors.[1]

After several additional millenia, civilization spread to western Europe, accompanied in its latter stages by the newly established Christian Church. Here the remaining areas of wilderness came to be viewed as places of potential danger, home to wild animals, demons, werewolves, semihuman wildmen, and pagans. The many references to wilderness in the Old and New Testaments of the Bible were ambiguous; the wilds were depicted as a place of hardship and testing, but they also could be the setting for spiritual communion and renewal. During the Middle Ages, as their populations increased, the Europeans cleared much of their forest wilderness. The thinning, and thus "civilizing," of the forests took away much of their perceived menace.[2]

When the first Europeans reached the shores of present-day Canada and the United States, they were met by a seemingly endless expanse of forest wilderness not unlike the former wilds of their Old World lands. This setting resurrected some of the feelings about wilderness which went back to the beginnings of civilization. The dark woods presented both real and imagined dangers, from the native population and from the wild animals.[3]

The Native Americans in this vast North American woodland wilderness may have numbered no more than one or two million, although some estimates are considerably higher. In the 1600s, during the age of colonization along the Atlantic coast, the countries of England, Sweden, the Netherlands, Spain, and France competed for land. The English eventually took over what had been the Swedish and Dutch colonies; Spain was unable to move north beyond the Florida region. This left the English and the French vying for control of most of what is now the eastern United States and Canada.

The French had settled in Canada in small towns along the St. Lawrence River during the early 1600s. Trading European goods to the Indians in order to obtain furs for export to France quickly became an essential part of the economy of this colony called New France. From there, a significant number of individuals, known as coureurs de bois (fur traders and trappers) and voyageurs (those who manned the canoes and boats), roamed the Great Lakes region and all along the Mississippi River and its tributaries. By trading with the Indians, and also by trapping, these Frenchmen acquired the furs needed to take back to the settlements. For many, however, this enterprise was simply a means to an end; it enabled them to enjoy the exhilarating freedom of the woods. The way in which these men took to the forests is noteworthy, because the relatively civilized conditions in France at that time were in sharp contrast to the untamed wildness of North America. Living for extended periods among the woodland Indians, many of these French rovers developed a true affinity for the wilds. The continuation of both their life in the forests and the fur trade on which all of New France depended would require the preservation of that wilderness.

When the English began colonizing in the early 1600s, their attitude toward the wilderness was very different from that of the French. Most of the English, basing their economy primarily on agriculture, fishing, commerce, and the shipping trade, remained concentrated near the coast in their colonies stretching from Massachusetts to the Carolinas. Slowly moving inland, they methodically destroyed the forests as they cleared land for crops. Although some individuals hunted in the surrounding woods, no significant numbers moved off permanently into the wilds. Some Englishmen did enter the fur trade, particularly in New York, Pennsylvania, and South Carolina, but it was of less overall importance than in New

France. Thus, in general, English colonists during this early period did not embrace the wilderness readily, and only sporadic and limited efforts were made at long-range penetration of the forest interior.

The hunting pioneer families, who would become a dynamic force in the English colonies by accelerating the movement westward into the wilderness, were the product of a special combination of cultures and circumstances. Never was there a better example of a people seizing an opportunity to fill a relatively fleeting ecological niche. Two main European groups stand out in the evolution of these ultimate backwoodsmen: the Swede-Finns and the Scotch-Irish. The intrinsic characteristics of these two groups would predominate among the hunting pioneers, although people of other European backgrounds would be represented in the ranks of these frontier families.

The Swede-Finns received their hyphenated designation by virtue of their being a Finnish people who, beginning in the late 1500s, moved from their homeland in the eastern interior forests of Finland to the wooded wilderness of central Sweden. From there in the mid-1600s, some of them migrated to the short-lived colony of New Sweden. This area in present-day New Jersey, eastern Pennsylvania, and northern Delaware soon would become part of English colonial America. Although small in numbers, the Swede-Finns would have a major impact on the woodland frontier lifestyle from the Atlantic Coast to the eastern edge of the Great Plains.

Unlike most other Europeans, who migrated to the New World from forest- and game-depleted lands, the Swede-Finns already were familiar with woodland pioneering and big game hunting from their experiences in the still thickly wooded climes of Finland and Sweden. Once in the New World, the Swede-Finns spread out in the sylvan wilderness along the lower Delaware River and its tributaries. Among the well-established customs and folkways which they brought with them from the Old World forests were: 1) hunting game such as deer and bear; 2) planting subsistence-type, small-scale crops in clearings created with ax and fire; 3) allowing their livestock to roam and forage through the woods; 4) settling in a dispersed and isolated manner; 5) building lean-tos for temporary hunters' camps (the warmth of the fire on the open side was reflected downward and to the rear under a slanting roof); and 6) constructing the style of log cabin which would become the typical frontier dwelling.[4]

In the New World wilderness, the Swede-Finns mingled with the Delaware Indians, learning about the wild foods available in the woods, incorporating native crops into their small-scale farming methods, and adapting to local hunting conditions. Terry G. Jordan and Matti Kaups, in *The American Backwoods Frontier: An Ethnic and Ecological Interpretation*, write that the transferral of such useful backwoods knowledge from the Indians to the Europeans began in earnest on this New Sweden frontier and was accomplished for the most part before the arrival, in large numbers, of other groups into the Delaware Valley. This combined Swede-Finn and Indian backwoods lifestyle would influence greatly other people on the frontier, including some English and Germans, but particularly the Scotch-Irish.[5]

The second European group of major importance in the history of the hunting pioneers was the Scotch-Irish. Although figures are inexact, by the outbreak of the Revolutionary War estimates place their numbers in the thirteen colonies at a quarter of a million, a significant percentage of the total population of two and a half million. Among the hunting pioneers, in particular, the Scotch-Irish would make up the great majority. Like the Swede-Finns, the Scotch-Irish acquired a hyphenated name from their involvement with two Old World countries, in this case Scotland and Ireland.

The Scotch-Irish who arrived in America were Scottish people migrating from northern Ireland where they had lived for decades after leaving their native Scotland in the 1600s. Throughout history, Scotland had been the scene of feuding, violence, and warfare, among the Scots themselves, as well as between the Scots and the English. Finally, by 1600, England had been able to impose a measure of order and control over its northern neighbor. Both England and Scotland had gone through the Reformation; most of the English had become Anglicans, and the majority of Scots in the lowlands embraced the Presbyterian faith. Wanting to strengthen their hold on Catholic Ireland, the English had encouraged many of the Protestant Scots to migrate to northern Ireland in the early 1600s. There they could continue to herd sheep and raise crops as they had done in Scotland for generations. Today, these people usually are referred to as Scotch-Irish, in order to differentiate them from the Scots who remained in Scotland and from the native Irish of Ireland.[6]

In northern Ireland, large numbers of the migrating Scots soon displaced the native Irish as the dominant landowners. Not surprisingly, over the years the Irish responded to this intrusion with a combination of sullen compliance, strong resistance, and bitter uprisings. In the 1600s, thousands on both sides perished during decades of fighting, warfare in which the English also became embroiled. Despite the turmoil, the Scotch-Irish managed to prosper to some extent economically through agriculture, sheep raising, and the woolen industry.[7]

As the years went by, however, the English government placed more and more restrictions on the woolen trade of the Scotch-Irish and on their Presbyterian religion.

These measures were taken with the objectives of reducing competition with the English woolen trade and converting the Scotch-Irish to the Anglican faith. Adding to these hardships, in northern Ireland there were low wages, high rents, and onerous taxes, as well as extreme shortages of food at times. These factors motivated great numbers of the Scotch-Irish to migrate to America, particularly to Pennsylvania, in the early decades of the 1700s. The majority of these newcomers appear to have been from the poorer classes, but the lack of material possessions did not affect their strong, stubborn pride. Finding that they did not fit in with the established society along the eastern seaboard, most of these Scotch-Irish quickly moved toward the western edges of settlement and beyond. Along the way, they came in contact with the Swede-Finns who, with some other pioneers in the Pennsylvania backwoods, had been perfecting an American wilderness lifestyle, part European and part Indian.[8]

Although neither Scotland nor Ireland possessed large expanses of heavily forested wilds by this time, something in the temperament of the Scotch-Irish would turn many of these immigrants into avid, wilderness-seeking, frontier people. Among the factors, no doubt, was their acclimatization to violence, warfare, struggle, and hardship, all of which had characterized life in Scotland and Ireland for generations. This background seems to have developed in these individuals great courage, hardiness, determination, and self-reliance. In addition, their long tradition of livestock herding may have created in many of the Scotch-Irish an aversion to extensive farming and predisposed them to take up a more unsettled life upon their arrival in America. (It should be noted, however, that the Scotch-Irish people would succeed to an outstanding degree in *all* aspects of American life, with several attaining the Presidency of the United States.)[9]

The Scotch-Irish who migrated to the Pennsylvania frontier soon showed a proclivity for "squatting," occupying land without purchasing it. When authorities would come to evict them, these squatters often resisted. If forced to leave, they soon would return. This behavior earned the Scotch-Irish a reputation among government officials as impetuous, audacious, contentious, and disorderly.[10]

By the 1730s, the Scotch-Irish were advancing into the wilderness in two directions. Some were moving west within Pennsylvania; others were following the southwestward curve of the Appalachians and heading into the backcountry of Maryland and Virginia. In so doing, both groups suddenly were placing themselves much further inland than most of the English colonists who were pushing the agricultural frontier more systematically westward from the coastal regions. By moving to the forefront of the advancing frontier, the Scotch-Irish, particularly those who were hunting pioneers, now stood on its cutting edge. They were joined by smaller numbers of Swede-Finns, English, and Germans. The Germans had been migrating to America in large numbers during this period, primarily due to devastating warfare in their homeland. A much smaller percentage of English and Germans became hunting pioneers compared to the Scotch-Irish and Swede-Finns. At the same time, all four of these groups would contribute to the ranks of the farming pioneers as the frontier moved westward.[11]

It had taken more than a century from the founding of the first English settlements along the Atlantic Coast for pioneers to reach part way toward the Appalachian Mountains. Now, suddenly, there was a major migration of people moving toward the far frontier. By 1730, the area which is known as the Valley of Virginia was playing a special role in this wilderness movement. This two-hundred-mile, north-south depression ran near the current western boundary of Virginia between the main chain of the Appalachian Mountains on the west and the Blue Ridge Mountains on the east. After frontier people began settling on lands at the northern end of this broad valley, each succeeding wave of pioneers moved further south, often making great advances beyond the last cabins. About a decade later, large numbers of both hunting pioneers and farming pioneers would leave behind a great stretch of newly inhabited land and move on from the lower end of the valley into southwestern Virginia. From there some of them would head toward the frontier of North Carolina.[12]

In the meantime, pioneer families had been moving into the backcountry of Virginia and North Carolina from the eastern portions of those colonies. Most of these people were recent Scotch-Irish and German immigrants; smaller numbers were native colonials, primarily English. Even at this early stage, these backwoods inhabitants with their dependence on hunting were being judged by travelers on the frontier. In 1728, William Byrd, a Virginia aristocrat, wrote in *The History of the Dividing Line*, "I am sorry to say it, but idleness is the general character of the men in the southern parts of this colony as well as in North Carolina. The air is so mild and the soil so fruitful that very little labor is required to fill their bellies, especially where the woods afford such plenty of game. These advantages discharge the men from the necessity of killing themselves with work, and then for the other article, of raiment, a very little of that will suffice in so temperate a climate. But so much as is absolutely necessary falls to the good women's share to provide. They all spin, weave, and knit, whereby they make good shift to clothe the whole family; and to their credit be it recorded, many of them do it very completely and thereby reproach their husbands' laziness in the most inoffensive way, that is to say, by discovering a better spirit of industry in themselves."[13]

During the 1730s and 1740s, Scotch-Irish, Swede-Finn, English, and German hunting pioneers were moving into the Virginia and North Carolina backcountry in increasing numbers. In 1749, Leonhard Schnell and John Brandmueller, Moravian missionaries who had arrived from Europe a few years earlier, described a portion of their journey on the Virginia frontier: "In the evening we lodged in an English cabin (thus they call the English houses there). It was quite cold. But the bear skins upon which we rested and the fire before us which kept us warm, rendered us good services. We had yet a piece of bread left, and as the people had none, we divided it with them. They gave us some of their bear meat, which can be found in every house in this district."[14]

Proceeding on their journey, three days later the missionaries again sought shelter for the night. "Then we came to a house, where we had to lie on bear skins around the fire like the rest. The manner of living is rather poor in this district. The clothes of the people consist of deer skins. Their food of Johnny cakes, deer and bear meat. A kind of white people are found here, who live like savages. Hunting is their chief occupation."[15]

Among the migrating pioneers during this period was Daniel Boone, destined to become the most famous of all the individuals who spent at least a portion of their lives as hunting pioneers. Born in 1734, Boone was descended from English Quakers who had migrated from England early in the 1700s and settled in Pennsylvania. Growing up in the eastern section of that colony, Boone spent much of his boyhood roaming the woods and hunting. Boone's father had a falling out with his fellow Quakers during the 1740s, and in 1750 the family departed from eastern Pennsylvania and joined the flood of pioneers moving southwestward. The Boones stayed for a time in the western Virginia wilderness, where young Daniel took off with a friend on his first extended hunting expedition. Roaming the Shenandoah and Blue Ridge Mountains, they were rewarded for their efforts with a large number of furs and hides.[16]

Resuming their migration, the Boones finally settled at the forks of the Yadkin River in the wilderness of west-central North Carolina. Many of the frontiersmen here spent a major amount of their time hunting, and the women and children tended to whatever crops were raised. Livestock, for the most part, ran wild in the woods. Boone, then in his late teens, helped his father with growing crops, but he had a great dislike for such work and wanted only to be out in the woods hunting. In addition to providing food for the table, the pursuit of wild game was quite profitable. Hunting would become Boone's chief livelihood and his primary occupation during the following three decades. The Upper Yadkin country teemed with wild game, particularly bear and deer. Boone was reputed to have killed ninety-nine bears along one creek in one season. As a result of this activity, he quickly became known for his hunting ability and marksmanship.[17]

The French and Indian War, which began in 1755, radically changed conditions on the western frontier. British General Edward Braddock's army was defeated overwhelmingly in July of that year by French-led Indians near recently built Fort Duquesne at present-day Pittsburgh. The effect of this severe loss was calamitous for the hunting pioneers and farming pioneers in the backcountry of Pennsylvania, Maryland, and Virginia. As the remnants of Braddock's command hastily returned to the East, the now unprotected pioneer families were highly vulnerable. The Indians soon struck, sometimes accompanied by the French. They left behind utter havoc and destruction. Hundreds of men, women, and children were killed or captured in sudden raids on their cabins. The frontier people were totally unprepared for this onslaught. There had been a long period of relative peace on the western frontier; also, by this time most of these pioneers were two or more generations removed from the harsh conflicts fought in their Old World homelands during the 1600s. In addition, at this point many of the hunting pioneers and farming pioneers had not yet developed their ultimate frontier characters and skills. Although some pioneers converted existing dwellings into private forts and stood their ground, large numbers of other backwoods families quickly fled eastward. Authorities soon built regular forts in an attempt to provide perimeters of defense, but offensive operations by the pioneers themselves normally were not even considered. However, in this long and brutal conflict, some of the frontiersmen would be able to match the backwoods fighting prowess of the Indians. This ability was demonstrated in the successful raid by three hundred backwoodsmen on the Indian town of Kittanning in western Pennsylvania in 1756. In 1758, a large British and colonial army advancing toward the site of Braddock's defeat forced the French to abandon Fort Dusquesne and at the same time virtually ended Indian raids and attacks on the frontiers of Pennsylvania, Maryland, and Virginia.[18]

Boone had traveled north from his home to serve as a wagon driver in the ill-fated Braddock campaign; he was among those fortunate enough to escape with their lives. Returning to North Carolina, he married Rebecca Bryan in 1756. His first two sons were born in 1757 and 1759, and for the most part he continued to depend on the proceeds gained from his hunting to support his growing family. The effects of the French and Indian War were spreading south, however, as the Cherokee became increasingly active against the frontiers of the Carolinas. By 1760, most of the pioneers in the Yadkin Valley, including Boone and his family, had retreated eastward for safety. Leaving his family secure, Boone later returned to the frontier where he was among the backwoodsmen participating with British and colonial troops in campaigns against the Cherokee. Here again some of the frontiersmen displayed their growing wilderness fighting skills.[19]

In the end, it was the determined efforts of the British Army which won the French and Indian War, with some aid from the colonials in the East and from the pioneers on the frontier. As a result of the defeat of France in the war, the French were forced to relinquish their holdings in North America in 1763. The removal of the French as a threat on the frontier added impetus to the westward expansion of the English colonies.

Charles Woodmason, an Englishman, was among the travelers who recorded their opinions of the hunting pioneers and other backwoods people during the decade following the French and Indian War. An itinerant Anglican minister, Woodmason journeyed extensively throughout the backcountry of South Carolina conducting religious services from 1766 to 1774. He tells of a trip during which he became lost, "wandering a Day and Night in the Wilderness, not knowing where I was," without any food. "Thus You have the Travels of a Minister in the Wild Woods of America. . . . Obliged to fight his Way thro' Banditti, profligates, Reprobates and the lowest vilest Scum of Mankind . . . ."[20]

Woodmason further characterizes the inhabitants: "And many live by Hunting, and killing of Deer—There's not a Cabbin but has 10 or 12 Young children in it—When the Boys are 18 and Girls 14 they marry—so that in many Cabbins You will see 10 or 15 Children. Children and Grand Children of one Size—and the mother looking as Young as the Daughter."[21]

These frontier people have many shortcomings, according to Woodmason. They are poor, ignorant, and lazy. Their numerous vices include "Licentiousness, Wantonness, Lasciviousness, Rudeness, Lewdness and Profligacy . . . ."[22]

Woodmason writes, "The Young Women have a most uncommon Practise, which I cannot break them off. They draw their Shift as tight as possible to the Body, and pin it close, to shew the roundness of their Breasts, and slender Waists (for they are generally finely shaped) and draw their Petticoat close to their Hips to shew the fineness of their Limbs—so that they might as well be in Puri Naturalibus—Indeed Nakedness is not censurable or indecent here, and they expose themselves often quite Naked, without Ceremony—Rubbing themselves and their Hair with Bears Oil and tying it up behind in a Bunch like the Indians—being hardly one degree removed from them."[23]

In *Unification of a Slave State: The Rise of the Planter Class in the South Carolina Backcountry, 1760-1808*, Rachel N. Klein points out that leaders in eastern South Carolina, as well as farming pioneers in that colony's backcountry, thought hunting pioneers were little different from the Indians in their lifestyle. Their habit of roaming and hunting was considered indolent compared to the labor required of people who followed agricultural pursuits. Hunting pioneers were accused of wantonly killing game, thus exacerbating tensions with the Indians. Hunting pioneers and farming pioneers in this backcountry region were not always completely distinct groups; some of the farming pioneers at times could be forced by circumstances to depend primarily on hunting for subsistence. Nevertheless, contemporaries in this area still saw a clear difference between those who were the real hunting pioneers and those who were not.[24]

Klein notes that a portion of the hunting pioneer

population in the South Carolina backcountry engaged in banditry, including the rustling of horses, cattle, and hogs. Some hunting pioneers, who themselves did not engage in such outlawry, aided or supported bandits. Both hunting pioneers and bandits shared a common resentment of established frontier society. Some farming pioneers on this untamed frontier also engaged in banditry.[25]

J. Hector St. John de Crevecoeur, who was quoted in the previous chapter, wrote as follows of the backcountry frontier during this period following the French and Indian War: "But to return to our back settlers. I must tell you, that there is something in the proximity of the woods, which is very singular. It is with men as it is with the plants and animals that grow and live in the forests; they are entirely different from those that live in the plains. . . . By living in or near the woods, their actions are regulated by the wildness of the neighbourhood." Often deer eat their grain, wolves attack their sheep, bears kill their hogs, and foxes catch their poultry. "This surrounding hostility immediately puts the gun into their hands; they watch these animals, they kill some; and thus by defending their property, they soon become professed hunters; this is the progress; once hunters, farewell to the plough. The chase renders them ferocious, gloomy, and unsociable; a hunter wants no neighbour, he rather hates them, because he dreads the competition."[26]

According to Crevecoeur, the deportment of the Indians was more respectable than the behavior of the hunting pioneers. The lifestyle of the latter brings on a new set of manners which produces "a strange sort of lawless profligacy," which creates an indelible impression. "Their wives and children live in sloth and inactivity; and having no proper pursuits, you may judge what education the latter receive. . . . To all these reasons you must add, their lonely situation, and you cannot imagine what an effect on manners the great distances they live from each other has!" This "unlimited freedom of the woods" has a great influence on them. "Eating of wild meat, whatever you may think, tends to alter their temper: though all the proof I can adduce is, that I have seen it: and having no place of worship to resort to, what little society this might afford is denied them. . . . Thus our bad people are those who are half cultivators and half hunters; and the worst of them are those who have degenerated altogether into the hunting state."[27]

People who till the earth, Crevecoeur states, are able to satisfy their material needs; also, because their time is divided between long hours of work and the necessary rest, they are too busy to commit "great misdeeds." With hunters, on the other hand, time is "divided between the toil of the chase, the idleness of repose, or the indulgence of inebriation. Hunting is but a licentious idle life, and if it does not always pervert good dispositions; yet, when it is united with bad luck, it leads to want: want stimulates that propensity to rapacity and injustice, too natural to needy men, which is the fatal gradation."[28]

Crevecoeur notes that because of the hunting life "the backsettlers of both the Carolinas, Virginia, and many other parts, have been long a set of lawless people; it has been even dangerous to travel among them. Government can do nothing in so extensive a country, better it would wink at these irregularities, than that it should use means inconsistent with its usual mildness. Time will efface those stains: in proportion as the great body of population approaches them they will reform, and become polished and subordinate."[29]

Following the French and Indian War, the forks of the Yadkin area in the North Carolina backcountry filled again with frontier people, including the Boone family. A direct result of the steadily increasing population in this region was the depletion of wild game. Consequently, Boone was venturing ever further from home, hunting in the mountains of present-day western North Carolina, southwestern Virginia, and eastern Tennessee. During the ensuing years, he roamed this area with other hunters or by himself, being away for weeks at a time. Boone considered hunting of much greater importance to his growing family's livelihood than any raising of crops. In 1766, in order to be closer to prime hunting ground, he moved west with his wife and children further up the Yadkin River.[30]

The Watauga, Holston, Nolichucky, Clinch, Powell, and French Broad river valleys of present-day northeastern Tennessee and adjacent southwestern Virginia have a special place in the history of westward migration. This region began gaining large numbers of hunting pioneer and farming pioneer families in the late 1760s. The strategic location of this area made it, along with the region surrounding the forks of the Ohio River, the great staging ground for subsequent movement throughout the Trans-Appalachian frontier. Boone moved his family there from the Yadkin River for a time during this period.[31]

In 1763, by establishing a Proclamation Line, the British government had made an unsuccessful attempt to keep pioneers from crossing the Appalachian Mountains and stirring up trouble with the Indians. Five years later, finally realizing the futility of trying to hold this line, authorities negotiated the Treaty of Hard Labor with the Cherokee for an adjustment of boundaries further westward into what is now West Virginia. Significantly, the treaty did not address the problem of pioneers moving onto Indian lands in present-day northeastern Tennessee. A Cherokee chief sent the following communication to the British Indian agent in 1769: "Father: The white people pay no attention to the talks we have had.

They are in bodies hunting in the Middle of our Hunting Grounds. Some of our people went as far as Long Island [of the Holston River], but were obliged to come Home, for the whole Nation is filling with Hunters, and the Guns rattling every way on the path, both up and down the River. They have settled the Land a great way this side of the line."[32]

In the meantime, during the early 1760s, a colorful group known as long hunters (because of their lengthy hunting trips) had appeared on the scene. In *The Long Hunt: Death of the Buffalo East of the Mississippi River*, Ted Franklin Belue refers to the long hunters as the freest individuals on the Anglo-American frontier before the Revolutionary War. Mark A. Baker, in *Sons of a Trackless Forest: The Cumberland Long Hunters of the Eighteenth Century*, states that the long hunters probably were the most talented and independent of any frontiersmen. The term long hunter is primarily associated with those individuals who traveled overland with packhorses across the Appalachian Mountains into the Kentucky and Tennessee country. However, they soon were joined by other frontiersmen who were supplied by Pennsylvania-based trading companies newly operating out of the Illinois country. These frontiersmen, originating primarily from southwestern Pennsylvania and northwestern Virginia, traveled from the Illinois region to the Kentucky and Tennessee country in log dugout canoes or in larger rivercraft known as batteaus. Because both the overland and the river-borne groups were leading similar lives while immersed in the wilderness, all of them will be referred to as long hunters in the descriptions which follow. Although they would be active for little more than a decade, these long hunters were destined to make an indelible mark in the annals of the frontier.[33]

To a large extent, the long hunters were an offshoot of the much larger population of hunting pioneers. The skills they required were common to both groups: marksmanship, tracking, stalking, trapping, preparing pelts, repairing equipment, caring for livestock, building shelters, preparing food, and administering remedies for sickness or injury. However, there were two distinguishing features which specifically applied to long hunters: 1) they were leaving their families far behind to go hunting for long periods; and 2) they were making their extended forays solely for market hunting.[34]

It is impossible to know how many long hunters came from the ranks of the hunting pioneers and how many came from the farming pioneers. Yet, simple logic would lead to the conclusion that those with a hunting pioneer background, including the propensity toward roving, would have been more inclined to undertake such extended expeditions. Nevertheless, some farming pioneers also would have acquired most of the requisite skills for long hunting simply by growing up in the backcountry, and certain of them may have been tempted to enter this activity for the potential profit. Although long hunting generally offered material rewards exceeding those of subsistence hunting or farming, the calling made few men much more than an adequate return for their efforts. Long hunting normally was not the path to easy wealth.[35]

The long hunters were able to enter the central Kentucky and Tennessee country, in particular, because no Indian tribes then inhabited it. However, several northern and southern tribes did utilize the area as a hunting ground. Along with the deep forests, this region contained extensive prairies, called barrens by early travelers, as well as large sections of canebrakes.

The long hunters brought with them what supplies and equipment they needed, including dried corn, salt, coffee, tobacco, gunpowder, lead, axes, and traps; as always, rifles and knives were close at hand. The corn was meant only to supplement their primary diet of meat, with deer, bear, wild turkey, buffalo, elk, and beaver being the most frequent entrees on their menu. Nuts and berries gathered in the woods added to their fare.[36]

For the most part, the size of the long hunter parties would dictate operations and logistics. These groups usually ranged from two or three men to a dozen or more. Often a base camp would be established, with many of the hunters splitting up and working out of outlying camps. The typical shelter was the open-faced lean-to; in addition, caves, overhanging rock ledges, tarps, and even hollow trees might be utilized. These camps would be vacated after an area had been hunted for a time, and new ones would be established.[37]

The hides of buffalo, elk, and bear were too bulky to carry out in large quantities, so deer hides and the furs of beaver and otter were favored by the long hunters. Sometimes there was a division of labor. The better hunters and trappers would bring in the pelts; others would prepare the hides and furs and then store them on scaffolds. Later, the pelts would be baled, and the men would convey them by either packhorse or rivercraft. The long hunters traveling on the rivers also were able to transport heavy casks of preserved meat, buffalo tallow, and bear oil.[38]

The lack of resident tribes in the region, along with an absence of open warfare at this time, gave the long hunters some freedom to roam widely. Nevertheless, there still was the danger of being discovered by unfriendly Indians moving through the area. When two or more men were hunting together, they normally refrained from firing their weapons at the same time in order to have at least one loaded rifle available. When circumstances appeared particularly dangerous, long hunters would spend the night hidden in the thick canebrakes through which not even an Indian could move without making noise.[39]

Daniel Boone was among the scores of long hunters who roamed the immense wilderness beyond the Appalachian Mountains. In 1769, Boone and five others set off for the Kentucky region, following the trail which would take them through the Cumberland Gap. Destined to become the primary overland route into the Trans-Appalachian region for hundreds of thousands of pioneers during the next half-century, this deep pass through the Cumberland Mountains is located at the point where the present-day states of Virginia, Kentucky, and Tennessee meet. Boone was gone a full two years during this extended hunting expedition. Twice, he and his party were confronted by Indians who confiscated their pelts. He later would indicate that, despite the dangers, this was among the most enjoyable times of his life.[40]

Boone was the only one of his group of long hunters who stayed out the entire two years. Lured on by the endless expanse of wilderness and the pure exhilaration of seeing new country, he had exhibited a great reluctance to return to civilization. In a book written by early Kentucky historian John Filson, Boone is purported to have said the following regarding this period in the wilds: "I had gained the summit of a commanding ridge, and, looking round with astonishing delight, beheld the ample plains, the beauteous tracts below. On the other hand, I surveyed the famous river Ohio that rolled in silent dignity, marking the western boundary of Kentucke with inconceivable grandeur. At a vast distance I beheld the mountains lift their venerable brows, and penetrate the clouds. All things were still." Further on in Filson's account, Boone is supposed to have remarked, "No populous city, with all the varieties of commerce and stately structures, could afford so much pleasure to my mind, as the beauties of nature I found here." Although the exact phrasing doubtless owes more to

Filson than to Boone, it is probable that the words paralleled the thoughts of the intrepid frontiersman. Boone himself claimed that Filson's book portrayed him in a completely accurate manner.[41]

Boone was so enamored of the Kentucky country that he decided to move there permanently. He was one of the leaders of a group of forty or fifty people, including his family and friends, who set off for the region in 1773. While enroute, his son, James, and two others went back for additional supplies. After obtaining the goods and reinforcing their contingent by several men, they started westward again to catch up with the main party. Detected by Indians, four of the group were killed, including Boone's son, who first was tortured. Greatly disheartened when they learned of this tragic event, the entire party turned back east, although Boone himself would have preferred that they continue westward. It would not be until two years later that Boone and other pioneers would locate permanently in the Kentucky region.[42]

The era of the long hunters, which began in the early 1760s, was virtually over by the opening of Lord Dunmore's War in 1774. That conflict, and the quickly following Revolutionary War and its aftermath, would make extended hunting expeditions in the Kentucky and Tennessee region too dangerous. By the time peace returned in 1794, the great population increases (which, surprisingly, had occurred despite the hostilities) prevented a resumption of long hunting. In contrast, the lifestyle of the hunting pioneer families with their smaller-scale hunting would be possible for a time in the Kentucky and Tennessee region before they would be forced to move on again into new wilderness.

In the meantime, further to the north, many hunting pioneers and farming pioneers had moved westward across Pennsylvania, Maryland, and northern Virginia to arrive in the region of Fort Pitt at present-day Pittsburgh by 1760. This English outpost replaced the earlier French Fort Duquesne on that site. Settling illegally along the Monongahela River south of Fort Pitt, the frontier people resisted the efforts of British soldiers to drive them off. In 1762, Colonel Henry Bouquet, the commander at Fort Pitt, wrote regarding these squatters, "For two years past these Lands have been over run by a Number of Vagabonds, who under pretense of hunting, were Making Settlements in several parts of them, of which the Indians made grievious and repeated Complaints," because such trespasses were in violation of an earlier treaty.[43]

The outbreak of Pontiac's Rebellion in 1763, coming on the heels of the recent French and Indian War, created chaos among the hunting pioneers and farming pioneers in the Fort Pitt region. Pontiac, an Ottawa chief, was one of the leaders of the defiant northern tribes who took part in this revolt. The reasons for this sudden uprising were many, including the growing presence of frontier people in the Fort Pitt area. A precipitating factor, however, was the new British policy ending the giving of gifts (including ammunition for hunting) to the tribes. The warriors achieved initial success by capturing most of the old French forts in present-day Ohio, Indiana, Michigan, and Wisconsin; these posts recently had been garrisoned by relatively small detachments of British soldiers. The majority of these forts were not seized by direct attacks but rather by means of ruses perpetrated against the often unsuspecting troops. This region north of the Ohio River had not been entered yet by hunting pioneers or farming pioneers. Just to the east in Pennsylvania, the frontier people in the area of Fort Pitt took refuge at that post or fled further eastward, as Indian raiding spread across the western backcountry of Pennsylvania, Maryland, and Virginia. As in the French and Indian War, these attacks were devastating. An estimated two thousand people on this long and exposed frontier were killed. Hundreds of others were captured. Fort Pitt and many smaller fortifications manned largely by pioneers withstood the onslaught until the British Army finally emerged victorious on the frontier. Although many of the backwoodsmen did not distinguish themselves during Pontiac's Rebellion, in that conflict some of them did prove their fighting skills in several sharp clashes with the Indians.[44]

A considerable number of the men, women, and children captured by the Native Americans in raids along the frontier had been spared either to be adopted into the tribe, held for ransom, or exchanged for Indians taken captive. As the tribes continually faced a severe population depletion, they felt it was necessary to replace deceased relatives with Indians captured from enemy tribes or with other people taken on the frontier. Interestingly, a significant portion of these latter individuals, from the ranks of the hunting pioneers and the farming pioneers, displayed a great reluctance to return to their former existence when given the opportunity. This phenomenon was observed in both males and females. Young children were the most easily assimilated. The Indians usually treated with great kindness those whom they adopted, and mutual bonds of affection often were established. In some cases, the adoptees married into the tribe. The unwillingness of many of these people to return to their former lives sometimes took an extreme form during exchanges of prisoners or ransoming of captives. Some individuals tried unsuccessfully to refuse repatriation, and many of them would run off later to rejoin the Indians in the wilderness. Such persons were referred to as "white Indians" by the society which they had rejected. Some boys and men even became "white renegades," actually joining the Indians in warfare against their own people.[45]

Benjamin Franklin earlier had speculated on the strong

appeal life in the wilderness held for both Indians and colonials. Writing to a friend in 1753, he commented that the "proneness of human nature to a life of ease, of freedom, from care and labour appears strongly in the little success that has hitherto attended every attempt to civilize our American Indians, in their present way of living, almost all their Wants are supplied by the spontaneous Productions of Nature, with the addition of very little labour, if hunting and fishing may indeed be called labour when Game is so plenty. . . ." Franklin notes that although the Indians frequently observe the advantages of colonial culture, they have no interest in emulating this lifestyle. "When an Indian Child has been brought up among us, taught our language and habituated to our Customs, yet if he goes to see his relations and make one Indian Ramble with them, there is no persuading him ever to return, and that this is not natural merely as Indians, but as men, is plain from this, that when white persons of either sex have been taken prisoner young by the Indians, and lived awhile among them, tho' ransomed by their Friends, and treated with all imaginable tenderness to prevail with them to stay among the English, yet in a Short time they become disgusted with our manner of life, and the care and pains that are necessary to support it, and take the first opportunity of escaping again into the Woods, from whence there is no reclaiming them."[46]

Some of the behavior shown by white captives, especially those who were taken at an early age or those who married into the tribe, could be attributed to emotional ties which had developed. But, as Franklin points out, another factor clearly was an attraction to the Indian wilderness lifestyle. It seems probable that the farming pioneer captives, in particular, would have embraced any opportunity to return to their earlier existence if living in the wilds had been unpleasant or abhorrent. Of course, almost all of the many captivity accounts which at one time formed an important genre of American literature were written by those former captives who were willing to leave the Indian life and return to their own people. Therefore, we have relatively little to tell us the other side of the story.

Perhaps the most eloquent characterization of those who wanted to stay permanently with the Indians was written by the nineteenth-century frontier historian Francis Parkman in *The Conspiracy of Pontiac and the Indian War after the Conquest of Canada*: "Among the captives brought in for delivery were some bound fast to prevent their escape; and many others, who, amid the general tumult of joy and sorrow, sat sullen and scowling, angry that they were forced to abandon the wild license of the forest for the irksome restraints of society." Parkman observes that a preference for the wilderness, where harsh conditions prevail with none of the supposed advantages of civilization, may seem strange; but this was the experience of many a healthful and sound mind. "To him who has once tasted the reckless independence, the haughty self-reliance, the sense of irresponsible freedom, which the forest life engenders, civilization thenceforth seems flat and stale. Its pleasures are insipid, its pursuits wearisome, its conventionalities, duties, and mutual dependence alike tedious and disgusting." (Probably neither the Indians nor the assimilated captives would have agreed with Parkman's use of the adjectives reckless, haughty, and irresponsible, but it seems likely they would have subscribed heartily to his general sentiments.) The person forced to be repatriated to civilized society cannot readjust; he grows restless and longs for "breathing room." The hardships and dangers suffered under primitive conditions had added spice to his life. "The wilderness, rough, harsh, and inexorable, has charms more potent in their seductive influence than all the lures of luxury and sloth." Those persons on whom the wilderness life "has cast its magic" cannot dissolve the spell, and they remain wanderers to the hour of their death.[47]

As soon as Pontiac's Rebellion ended in 1765, hunting pioneers as well as farming pioneers ventured out again into the Fort Pitt region. This expansion occurred despite the fact that the Proclamation Line of 1763, mentioned earlier, had been designed to keep them east of the Appalachian Mountains and thus prevent further trouble with the Indians. Once more, British troops from Fort Pitt were sent to drive back these frontier people. Their habitations were burned and their livestock seized. These squatters, however, exhibited a new level of tenacity and determination at the same time as their numbers were increasing. Evicted from one place, they quickly returned or sought another location nearby. This conduct indicated a new spirit of great determination and fortitude among these backwoods people.[48]

The renewed presence of squatters posed a threat to peace with the Indians. Thus, in 1768, as the Treaty of Hard Labor was being worked out with the Cherokee to the south, the British authorities in the north were negotiating the Treaty of Fort Stanwix with the important Iroquois Confederacy, whose once powerful influence over nearby tribes was in decline. The Treaty of Fort Stanwix moved the Proclamation Line of 1763 further westward to incorporate more of western Pennsylvania, as well as a portion of the Kentucky region. The Iroquois were willing to give up this land only because it was an area which they claimed but did not use. They conveniently overlooked the fact that their one-time tributary tribes, the Shawnee and Delaware, as well as the detached Iroquois group known as the Mingo, did use this area for hunting. All of these tribes lived in the nearby Ohio country. Angry at the actions of the Iroquois, whose legendary reputations as warriors they still respected, the tribes in the upper Ohio River country only reluctantly acquiesced in this cession of land, and only for a time.[49]

General Thomas Gage, the British commander in North America, referred to the individuals who were exerting pressure on Indian lands as "Lawless Banditti." In 1772, he wrote in a letter, "An Indian interpreter was here a few days past from the Ohio, who saw thirty or forty people seated on the banks of that river on the lands ceded by the Six Nations, and on whose approach some Indians in the neighbourhood abandoned their dwellings and removed. Many of those people were half-naked, chiefly covered with loose, coarse linen frocks such as the frontier people manufacture for themselves and paint or colour with bark, and they differ little from Indians in their manner of life." Gage states that the need to purchase clothing "induces them to hunt and consequently to intrude on the Indian hunting grounds," which often results in quarrels and murders.[50]

As the 1770s progressed, the continuing flow of hunting pioneers and farming pioneers into the Fort Pitt region (as well as the previously described entry of much smaller numbers of long hunters into what is now Kentucky and Tennessee), posed a direct threat to the Indians who lived in the Ohio country. Ironically, over the years the economies of the Indians and the pioneers had become more and more similar. In addition to relying on many of the same manufactured items, both groups engaged to varying degrees in hunting and crop raising, while also making use of horses, pigs, and cattle to some extent.[51]

With tensions growing, killings on both sides increased. In giving background information on this period, Lord Dunmore, governor of Virginia, wrote in a letter to the Earl of

Dartmouth in 1774, "But these new injuries stirred up the old inveteracy of those who are called the backwoodsmen, who are hunters like the Indians and equally ungovernable; these people took fire all along the frontiers quite to Maryland and Pennsylvania and formed parties avowedly against the Indians which the efforts of magistrates and government could not in the least restrain." In this letter, Dunmore also made what probably is his most quoted observation: "But, my lord, I have learnt from experience that the established authority of any government in America and the policy of government at home are both insufficient to restrain the Americans and that they do and will remove as their avidity and restlessness incite them. They acquire no attachment to place, but wandering about seems engrafted in their nature, and it is a weakness incident to it that they should forever imagine the lands further off are still better than those upon which they are already settled."[52]

Finally, relations between the Indians and the frontier people in the upper Ohio River region reached a critical juncture. The Shawnee, in particular, were determined to drive the intruders back, even though Iroquois pressure succeeded in keeping other tribes from openly joining them in any significant numbers. The Indians soon would discover, however, that the frontier people had developed a much greater determination to hold their ground and even undertake independent and large-scale offensive operations than they had shown in the past. The incredible horror and havoc they experienced in the French and Indian War and in Pontiac's Rebellion seemed to have forged a hardened and steely character in many of these pioneers. Both the hunting pioneers and the farming pioneers knew that they must defeat the Indians in order to achieve the peaceful conditions which would enable their respective lifestyles to continue and thrive. Therefore, before we can examine the years of optimum conditions for the hunting pioneer families, as documented in the extensive eyewitness accounts of travelers found in chapters 4, 5, and 6, we first must turn in Chapter 3 to the role of the hunting pioneers in frontier warfare.[53]

WILDERNESS WARFARE

Sudden death at the hands of an enemy was a stark reality for the hunting pioneers during much of their era. Therefore, no study of these people would be complete without a thorough look at the true nature of this deadly wilderness struggle. On the periphery of the American frontier, the hunting pioneers were in a particularly hazardous position in times of open hostility. During the latter stages of both the French and Indian War and Pontiac's Rebellion, the British Army did provide some measure of protection. By the early 1770s, all this had changed, however, as events in the East were leading inexorably to the outbreak of the War of American Independence. Soon, the frontiersmen would be fighting not only the Indians but the British as well. The Revolutionary War era on the frontier, the most outstanding illustration of extended woodland warfare, forms the centerpiece of this chapter. During this period, more of both the hunting pioneers and the farming pioneers would develop into steadfast and capable wilderness fighters.

In order to assess properly the role of the hunting pioneers in wilderness warfare, it is necessary to look first at their major opponents, the Native Americans. From the time of their initial contact, Europeans viewed the Indians of North America as destined for conquest by a superior culture. Native

Americans were considered to be savages, i.e., people living in "uncivilized" and "primitive" societies. This was true whether the Europeans viewed them as "noble savages" leading an ideal life in paradisiacal surroundings or as "ignoble savages" existing without social discipline in a realm of violence. Both of these views overlooked all the evidence: these diverse tribal societies actually featured very successful economies of hunting, fishing, and foraging, combined in many areas with highly developed agriculture, extensive intertribal trade, large population centers, and effective government.[1]

Accounts indicate that the Native Americans usually did not view with hostility the Europeans who first appeared in their lands. In fact, often the Indians were impressed initially with these strangers, sometimes even believing them to be godlike beings. This attitude was due, in part, to the awe with which the Indians beheld the seemingly miraculous possessions of the Europeans. In addition to their impressive ships, these people brought with them incredible and useful objects made of metal or cloth, which they often presented as gifts or used in bartering. In many first contacts, the Indians accorded the Europeans respect and courtesy, treating them as honored guests. They also dispensed information on how to survive in this new environment and furnished the newcomers with sorely needed provisions. Although the Europeans on the scene were well aware that it was the Native Americans' bountiful agricultural surplus which made possible this largess, Europeans in general still were inclined to categorize Indians as savages addicted only to the hunt.[2]

The Europeans had arrived in what is now the United States fully prepared for military action. Once they gained a foothold on these shores, they often killed the native inhabitants for real or imagined offenses. Indians also were taken into slavery. Conquest was made considerably easier by the fact that the tribes suffered catastrophic losses through diseases which were introduced into the New World by the Europeans. Despite these unfavorable circumstances, over the next two centuries the woodland Indians would put up a strong, tenacious, and deadly resistance. Such confrontations continued throughout the wilderness from the Atlantic coast to the edge of the Great Plains, until these forest-dwelling Indians finally were overcome. In this warfare, the native inhabitants proved themselves worthy opponents of all who came against them, including the hunting pioneers.[3]

Although there was some large-scale, intertribal conflict prior to the appearance of the Europeans, the tribes of what is now the eastern United States had carried on primarily small-scale, indecisive, and almost ritualistic combat. Early European military observers tended to view with amusement and contempt these seemingly casual and half-hearted engagements, which were in striking contrast to the carnage and slaughter often witnessed in the Old World. Suddenly caught up in a whirlwind of changes over which they appeared to have little or no control, soon many of the tribes were responding by vehemently striking out at their enemies. In so doing, they often targeted both the Europeans and their own traditional tribal foes in a manner which now matched the unlimited and uncompromising warfare practiced at times by the Europeans themselves. This warfare carried on by the Indians was made all the more effective by a deep-rooted familiarity with their wilderness surroundings, an almost intuitive understanding which they had acquired through untold generations. For most seventeenth-century Europeans, any idea they earlier had entertained of Indians as "noble savages" was replaced quickly with the "ignoble savage" concept when the Native Americans began to resist seriously the appropriation of their land. (As we shall see in Chapter 4, the "noble savage" concept would reappear in much more elucidated form a century later.)[4]

Many Europeans soon changed their opinion of the Native Americans' fighting ability and grudgingly came to admire the warriors' bravery, skill, and endurance. Others focused on the ruthlessness and cruelty of Indian warfare, although Europeans in America acted in the same manner. For example, the taking of scalps was a part of the culture of most tribes, predating the arrival of the Europeans, but the latter soon adopted the practice. Moreover, authorities in the colonies sometimes paid bounties for Indian scalps.[5]

It is not known when the Native American practice of inflicting prolonged and horrific torture on captives first appeared. Apparently, the Iroquois had been torturing their enemies before the advent of the Europeans, and this barbarity at times was reciprocated by other northeastern tribes. Yet, there are indications such torture may have been less frequent in other portions of the woodlands of North America when the tribes fought only among themselves. It is possible that some of the tribes finally started torturing Europeans in retaliation for similar treatment from these newcomers. Europeans had utilized torture during the Middle Ages in their own lands, where it included the burning of individuals at the stake. This form of torture by fire was used early by Europeans on Indian captives. However, at the same time that colonization was progressing, the infliction of such torment came to be viewed with growing disfavor in European society. It appears, therefore, that as the European practice of torture was diminishing, its use by the Indians seems to have been increasing. Ironically, this practice may have backfired on the Indians, because in many instances their adversaries fought furiously to the last breath rather than risk such a fate by surrendering.[6]

Despite the many skirmishes and battles fought by the Indians against the Europeans and the Americans, it is readily apparent with the benefit of hindsight that the tribes made three fundamental mistakes which ultimately proved their undoing. Their first error was not concentrating single-mindedly and without letup on expelling the newcomers once the latter's agenda had become apparent. Instead, the Indians were distracted from this goal by the continuation of their age-old intertribal wars. Thus, they failed to present a united front against the Europeans from the beginning. Exacerbating this disunity, tribes often enlisted the Europeans to assist them in making war on their hereditary enemies for whom they usually harbored hatred and animosity for past sufferings; conversely, the Indians also allowed themselves to be recruited by one colonial power or another to make war on a competing colonial power and that colony's Indian allies. Although through the years many of the tribes periodically united against the threat posed by the Europeans, and later the Americans, they continued this warfare among themselves to the very end. In *A Spirited Resistance: The North American Indian Struggle for Unity, 1745-1815*, Gregory Evans Dowd stresses the spiritual foundation of this elusive quest for Native American solidarity, which held that all Indians were a single people despite tribal divisions.[7]

The Indians' second major mistake, although fully understandable, was their pursuit of European manufactured goods which they thought would make their life in the wilderness easier and more comfortable. Knives, hatchets, kettles, and other items made of metal were a great advance over their own implements. Blankets, cloth, ornamental jewelry, and, unfortunately, alcohol were much sought after as well.

Firearms were the objects most coveted. In a culture

which exalted the successful hunter and warrior, the acquisition of these weapons was a prime goal. Indians quickly became highly proficient in their use and often were better marksmen than the Europeans. For hunting, an activity in which the speed of reloading usually was not a critical factor, the greater knockdown power of the early firearms could be seen as an advancement over the bow and arrow. In wilderness warfare, on the other hand, it is debatable whether the matchlock arquebus or even the later flintlock musket was superior to the bow. In close quarters combat, particularly, the bow might have been a better choice over these firearms, because numerous arrows could be launched in the time it took to reload a gun. In fighting at a longer range, however, the bow normally was inferior to firearms; arrows coming from a distance sometimes could be dodged, but lead balls could not. In intertribal warfare, interestingly, those tribes which did have firearms usually prevailed against those which did not, although the reason may have been partially psychological. The Indians used a combination of muskets and bows very effectively in ambushes, raids, and battles during a major war against the New England colonists in 1675 and 1676. Not surprisingly, as the years went by and firearms were acquired by more and more warriors, many of the Indians lost their earlier skills with the bow and arrow.[8]

An account written in 1728 by William Byrd, who was quoted in Chapter 2, notes how the Indians in their hunting and in their wars "now use nothing but firearms, which they purchase of the English for skins." Byrd states that it makes good sense for the English to sell firearms to the Indians, because the Indians then become dependent on the traders for their continued subsistence. Inferring that the warriors were having difficulty developing effective fighting tactics using guns alone, Byrd adds, "Besides, they were really able to do more mischief while they made use of arrows, of which they would let silently fly several in a minute with wonderful dexterity, whereas now they hardly ever discharge their firelocks more than once, which they insidiously do from behind a tree and then retire" as nimbly as European cavalry.[9]

Acquiring a liking for, and later a dependence on, trade items meant that the Native Americans had to maintain a friendly relationship with at least one colonial power. They were forced to increase greatly their killing of wildlife, because the pelts of these animals were the only items the Europeans wanted in trade. The Indians went from subsistence hunting, in which they had not depleted the wild game, to commercial or market hunting, in which some species of animals were slaughtered ruthlessly in order to obtain trade goods.

The first two major mistakes of the Indians led inevitably to the third. Under the unrelenting pressure of the European advance, tribes frequently negotiated away the lands they used and claimed, or sometimes the territory which in reality was used or claimed by another tribe. In return, they normally received trade goods. In some instances, Europeans dealt with those tribal leaders who were the most amenable to relinquishing land, ignoring those who were opposed. On other occasions, defeats in wars led to the loss of Indian land.

Warriors normally entered into major campaigns against the Europeans through the consensus of their tribal elders. Considerable planning, preparation, and discipline in execution went into these large-scale efforts. On the other hand, small-scale raiding activities often were the result of more informal recruitment by a leader with a reputation for fighting skills or successful military actions. Regardless of the type of operation to be undertaken, the Indians' main strategy in wilderness warfare was knowing when, and when not, to fight. They usually did not seek a confrontation, except when they held the advantage and could be assured of a victory without significant casualties; large losses would deplete seriously their limited populations. Lacking cannons, Indians often were reluctant to risk such losses by attempting to take a well-defended or fortified structure unless the warriors first could set it on fire.[10]

The Indians' greatest objective was to surprise or ambush their opponents without being surprised or ambushed themselves. This tactic was used in both large-scale warfare and in raiding. Able to traverse the woods for hundreds of miles with virtually no encumbrances, the warriors could emerge without warning at any point on the long frontier. By the time they first opposed the hunting pioneers in a major war in the 1750s, the Indians had improved and perfected their tactical use of flintlock muskets. Before the outbreak of the Revolutionary War in 1775, some of the warriors had acquired rifles, which further increased their capabilities. The Indians' method of launching an attack was singularly striking and effective, particularly in situations where the first few moments might decide the outcome. In such circumstances, their foes were met with a hail of lead sent from a position of total concealment. Then the warriors, their bodies painted with vivid colors and striking designs, would charge out from cover screaming soul-chilling war cries. They would endeavor to overpower their opponents' minds with fear and intimidation; if they were able to close with the enemy in this onrush, the Indians' weapon of choice would be the tomahawk.[11]

When engaged in more extended battles, the warriors would try quickly to outflank their opponents and partially or completely surround them, often in a halfmoon formation. Soon the Indians' adversaries would be receiving well-aimed fire from different directions. Fighting in a scattered fashion, the warriors were masters at using the available cover, as they took turns advancing and giving protective fire. If the situation looked favorable, they would make an all-out frontal assault in an attempt to overwhelm their opponents. When pressed by the enemy, they would fall back, only to return at the first opportunity. If the fighting was going against them, the Indians would melt away into the woods; when possible, they made every effort to carry off their wounded and dead. Through thousands of years of fighting in a woodland environment, the Indians had perfected the art of wilderness combat.[12]

To contend with their Indian opponents, the hunting pioneers and farming pioneers eventually would depend on the basic strategy used early on by the Europeans against the Native Americans in the coastal regions: total war, defensive when necessary, offensive when possible. This fighting usually exhibited shocking ferocity and brutality on both sides, with no quarter expected and none normally given. The Indians, viewing this conflict as a struggle to preserve their life in the wilds and even their very existence, considered both hunting pioneers and farming pioneers to be agents of their doom. Conversely, the hunting pioneers believed the Indians to be the major impediment to achieving their desired lifestyle in the wilderness, and the farming pioneers were anxious to destroy the same wilderness on which the other two groups depended, in order to make possible their own mode of living.

Over the years, many myths and legends have grown up regarding the wilderness fighting prowess of the American frontiersmen. Some of these stories are based on fact; others are not. The actual records show that the fighting capabilities of the pioneers ranged from poor to superior, but these accounts do not indicate clearly the difference between the wilderness martial abilities of the hunting pioneers and those of the farming pioneers. The hunting pioneers, however, by virtue of their almost incessant roaming and hunting on the extreme margins of the frontier, were more likely than the farming pioneers to have developed fully the skills needed in woodland warfare. These skills included woodcraft, stalking, and marksmanship. The lifestyle of the hunting pioneers also inured them to long-distance travel, extremes of weather, and the general privations experienced in wilderness hostilities. In addition, they often were familiar with the country to be traversed, making their services as guides and scouts particularly valuable.

During times of full-scale war, the distinctive differences in the lifestyles of hunting pioneers and farming pioneers diminished, as both groups were forced to modify their normal activities. The hunting pioneers usually found it necessary to pull back from their exposed locations and curtail their wilderness roving, and the farming pioneers often were unable to remain on their farms. As a result, both types of frontier people frequently gathered together in forts or stockaded stations of various sizes, or they moved eastward to larger settlements for the duration of the conflict.

Hunting pioneers, as well as other frontiersmen, could engage in woodland warfare in several ways: 1) as an individual; 2) as part of an informal or unorganized group; 3) as a member of the local militia (usually composed of all able-bodied men, sometimes from as young as fifteen years to as old as 50 or 60); and 4) as a member of a regular colonial or state force. Many of the large-scale frontier campaigns were carried out primarily by either conscripts or volunteers from the militia. Militia also manned forts. Men who were noted for their wilderness skills were frequently selected from the militia and employed as scouts or spies (the terms scouts and spies often were used interchangeably.)

Military leaders on the frontier tended to be of two types. First, there were individuals with wealth, position, or social prestige, some of whom moved to the frontier with strong connections to powerful families in the East; they often received their commands by appointment. Second, there were the men without upper-class advantages, who were elected to command primarily because of their demeanor, bravery, and wilderness fighting skills. In order for leaders from the first category to be fully effective, they had to possess many of the same attributes as those from the second category.[13]

In the period prior to 1787, the basic structure of government was extended to the frontier by the various original colonies or states through the creation of large new counties. After 1787, huge territories usually were established on the expanding frontier as a preliminary step to statehood. Military authority in all of these areas was quickly formalized by the organization of a militia. Field grade officers were given the ranks of colonel, lieutenant-colonel, and major; normally of the gentry, these men were selected by colonial, state, or territorial officials. In turn, these leaders often selected the company-level officers (captains and lieutenants), sometimes choosing relatives or younger members of their own class. It was at this point that controversy could occur. Although most frontiersmen conceded that they had little or no say in who occupied the higher ranks, periodically they might assert their preferences for company-level command. On occasion, they even declined to serve under an officer appointed by higher authorities, if the appointee was deemed unacceptable. Furthermore, if volunteers from the militia were needed for lengthy campaigns, some pioneers would decline to join the expedition if the reputation of the overall commander (usually a lieutenant-colonel or colonel, but occasionally a brigadier-general) did not meet their expectations.[14]

Early on, hunting pioneers and farming pioneers fought with muskets; after 1750, they increasingly used long rifles. In close-quarters combat, they wielded their large hunting knives. By the time of the Revolutionary War, the Indians frequently referred to the frontiersmen as the Long Knives or the Big Knives. Most backwoodsmen carried a tomahawk as an additional weapon. With the exception of some officers, frontier militia normally did not wear uniforms.

In the midst of the French and Indian War, wilderness "rules of war" had been encoded in the rugged mountain and forest wilds of upper New England, far to the north and east of the hunting pioneers who lived on the western frontier. Robert Rogers of New Hampshire had organized a formal military force of backwoodsmen, known as Rogers' Rangers, to combat the forays of the French and Indians in the no-man's-land of those northern forests. Although working in cooperation with the British Army, these rangers carried out successful offensive operations acting alone. To a large extent, Rogers' methods of conducting war followed those of the Indians. His tactics also were those which the hunting pioneers and farming pioneers on the western frontier would come to follow almost instinctively. In much abbreviated form, Rogers' rules included: marching in single file, keeping a good distance apart, with scouts in advance and flankers out to the sides; fighting the enemy by advancing from tree to tree; outflanking the adversary in battle; holding fire on an attacking enemy until the last moment, then rushing them in hand-to-hand combat; dispersing individually to gather later at a prearranged point if there is a danger of being surrounded; forming a circle if totally surrounded and then holding off the antagonists until darkness makes escape possible; not following in the tracks of an enemy if they are some distance ahead, but instead getting ahead of them by a parallel route and waiting for them in ambush; circling back on one's own tracks and setting up an ambush if pursued by a foe; and taking turns in dropping back to fire on pursuers if closely followed while retreating.[15]

During times of heightened tensions, frontier people lived with the knowledge that the next moment could bring an attack. The threat was present whether they were living in their cabins, staying at forts, or moving through the woods. This danger escalated in times of open warfare. The great majority of confrontations between frontiersmen and their enemies were small-scale incidents, many of them unrecorded at the time. Relived again and again in hearthside reminiscences, the facts of these events were susceptible of change or embellishment before finally being chronicled. With the element of surprise and the comparative numbers on each side frequently being the overriding and decisive factors from the onset of the action, the results of such encounters were not necessarily indicative of fighting skills. To gain the clearest assessment of the hunting pioneers' martial abilities, it is necessary to: 1) concentrate on the Revolutionary War era, by which time many more of the frontier people had evolved into proficient and aggressive combatants; 2) examine larger-scale clashes between forces of relatively equal size which were well-documented in journals, letters, or official reports shortly after the event; 3) include only those battles in which the element of surprise was not the sole or major determinant of the outcome; and 4) limit the review to those engagements in which it is certain a large number of hunting pioneers took part.

Both the times and the places of the following eleven confrontations ensure that a significant portion of the frontiersmen involved were hunting pioneers. Also, it was during these years that the frontier people normally fought their enemies with little help from the central government far to the east. These battles, their dates, and their locations are: 1) Battle of Point Pleasant, 1774 (West Virginia); 2) Battle of Long Island Flats, 1776 (Tennessee); 3) siege of Boonesborough,

1778 (Kentucky); 4) capture of Fort Sackville, 1779 (Indiana); 5) attack on the Shawnee, 1779 (Ohio); 6) attack on the Shawnee, 1780 (Ohio); 7) Battle of King's Mountain, 1780 (South Carolina); 8) attack on the Wyandot, 1782 (Ohio); 9) Battle of Blue Licks, 1782 (Kentucky); 10) attack on the Shawnee, 1782 (Ohio); and 11) attack on the Shawnee, 1786 (Ohio).

The Battle of Point Pleasant, fought between the frontiersmen and the Indians, took place a year before the American Revolution began. At that time, the attention of the British Army was focused primarily on the rapidly deteriorating relationship between England and the colonies in the East. British military leaders already had evacuated most of their frontier posts, including Fort Pitt, and concentrated their forces along the Atlantic seaboard; they had little interest in getting involved in a frontier war with the Indians. As described at the conclusion of Chapter 2, during this period there was a growing concern among the Shawnee, Delaware, and Mingo about the rapid increase of frontier people moving into the upper Ohio River and Kentucky regions. Tensions on both sides heightened, and the number of pioneers and Indians killed in random encounters mounted. The Iroquois, traditional allies of the English and earlier overlords of the tribes in the Ohio country, exerted pressure to keep those tribes from taking action. To a large extent, these efforts were successful with the Mingo and Delaware. The Shawnee, however, became increasingly hostile toward the frontiersmen. Daniel Boone and another hunter, because of their familiarity with the region, were dispatched to the Kentucky country in order to give warning of the potential peril to surveyors who had begun entering that area the previous year.[16]

Lord Dunmore, British governor of Virginia, was quick to react to the ominous situation on the frontier. Despite the storm clouds gathering in the East between England and the colonies, Dunmore was anxious to assert Virginia's claim to the region which is now western Pennsylvania and Kentucky. He realized that aid would not be forthcoming from the British Army. Even the militia in the eastern portion of Virginia could not be counted on to help; like the British Army, they had no interest in a frontier war. Dunmore turned instead to his militia commanders on the western frontier of Virginia. In 1774, he issued orders for two forts to be built on the upper Ohio River in what is now West Virginia. The northernmost fort was constructed at present-day Wheeling, and the other fort was to be erected two hundred miles to the southwest at the mouth of the Kanawha River. The hunting pioneers and farming pioneers who built the first fort soon launched a campaign against the Shawnee. Commanded by Major Angus McDonald, four hundred militia marched into the Ohio country wilderness in July 1774 and burned several of the Indian towns. They met only limited resistance from the Shawnee, who had been biding their time while still hoping to gain support from their Indian allies before starting a war.[17]

In the meantime, Colonel Andrew Lewis was raising a force of approximately one thousand hunting pioneers and farming pioneers from the militia in the southwestern counties of Virginia. His intention was not only to build the second fort as Dunmore had directed but also to launch an offensive campaign against the Indians. The book, *Gentry and Common Folk: Political Culture on a Virginia Frontier 1740-1789*, a study by Albert H. Tillson, Jr., focuses on the specific area of present-day southwestern Virginia from which the men for Lewis' campaign were recruited. Tillson notes that in the earlier military activities in this area during the French and Indian War, militia leaders had experienced trouble enforcing discipline; their men refused to perform military service, disobeyed orders, and deserted. In addition, many of the frontier people had fled eastward. Although there may have been less flight in 1774, Lewis' officers still found recruiting for the Point Pleasant campaign to be a problem. Some of this reluctance to serve was due to a concern many of the men had about leaving their families unprotected.[18]

Tillson writes that much of the dissension in the militia was caused by differing views of leadership. The gentry valued dignity, status, and a sense of authority in their leaders. The frontiersmen identified more closely with a person of stirring action. Lewis, a member of the gentry elite, was generally unpopular with the men because of his authoritarian and aloof manner. Not all gentry acted in this manner. Lewis' brother Charles, for example, was widely popular as an officer because of his reputation as an inspiring leader.[19]

Despite the less than total enthusiasm for the upcoming campaign, many of the local population exhibited the same martial spirit which had been evident in McDonald's recent expedition. Leaving their encampment at present-day Lewisburg, West Virginia, in early September 1774, Lewis' force proceeded on foot through the rugged wilderness. After a long and arduous trek, the army arrived on October 6 at the junction of the Kanawha and Ohio rivers, a location known as Point Pleasant. Here they learned that Dunmore, heartened by the response of the frontier militia, had taken to the field himself at the head of an enlarged northern contingent. His intention was to unite the two commands and lead them against the Shawnee in the Ohio country.[20]

The Shawnee, along with some Mingo and Delaware also defying the Iroquois edict, hoped to defeat Lewis' and Dunmore's forces in separate actions. Led by Chief Cornstalk, they decided to attack Lewis' army first. The total number of Indians involved is uncertain; it may have approximated the number of frontiersmen or been considerably less. Moving forward to attack in the early morning of October 10, the warriors were frustrated in their efforts to achieve complete surprise when they encountered some frontiersmen who were out hunting. Quickly the alarm was given, and thus began an all-day battle. Three hundred men who were sent out by Andrew Lewis to ascertain the situation received heavy fire. Charles Lewis was killed and another colonel seriously wounded, and their reconnaissance force was thrown back.[21]

As militia reinforcements arrived at the scene of the fighting, the frontiersmen slowly made the Indians give ground. At times, the fighting became intense and was carried on at close range. The battle lines eventually extended over a mile in length. The combatants on both sides fought from behind trees in the fashion typical of backwoods warfare. The diffuse nature of the fighting made any effective coordination difficult. Neither side ever launched an all-out assault. In addition, some of the frontiersmen never advanced far enough to take an active part in the battle.[22]

As the day wore on, the two sides stabilized their lines, and the struggle slackened in intensity. Toward nightfall, the Indians finally withdrew across the Ohio River. The frontiersmen suffered approximately two hundred killed and wounded, including an unusually high percentage of officers. Indian losses are uncertain, but they may have been somewhat comparable. The militia's retention of the field in the Battle of Point Pleasant gave them a claim to a crucial victory, in both real and psychological terms. As a result, the Shawnee elected to seek peace. At the treaty conference which concluded what came to be known as Lord Dunmore's War, the way was opened for an important movement of pioneers into the upper Ohio River and Kentucky regions in the critical period just prior to the War of American Independence. Because the victory at Point Pleasant was of such importance to the immediate future of the frontier, the encounter is sometimes referred to as the first battle of the American Revolution.[23]

Upon his return from warning the surveyors in Kentucky, Daniel Boone had wanted to join Andrew Lewis' expedition. Due to his growing reputation for wilderness skills and leadership ability, Boone instead was given command of several small forts in the Clinch River region of southwestern Virginia. Serving as a lieutenant, he was active in the defense of that area when a series of Indian raids and attacks took place there during Lord Dunmore's War. As a result of his services, he subsequently was promoted to captain.[24]

In *The American Revolution in Indian Country: Crisis and Diversity in Native American Communities*, Colin G. Calloway states that by 1775 the Indians already had undergone momentous change. After a century and a half of tremendous upheaval, their world bore little resemblance to that which had existed in pre-European times. In addition to the decimation of their numbers by disease and war, the Indians experienced a great mingling of peoples. Most of the tribes had been uprooted and intermixed. Also, there often were traders, missionaries, captives, and other Europeans who lived in the villages. The southern tribes had the additional influence of African Americans living in their midst as runaway slaves or captives. All of this intermingling led to the existence of people with mixed ancestry, many of whom became influential within the tribes. Furthermore, some of the Native Americans had been Christianized, which often created factions within the individual tribes. There also was a meshing of colonial and Indian economies, most notably in the fur trade. As a result, the Indians had become dependent to varying degrees on a large number of European manufactured goods.[25]

After the Revolutionary War began, the situation on the

frontier became even more unsettled, as both the British and the Americans sought to gain control of the vast region from the Appalachians westward. But it was the Indians who held the balance of power, because there were many more of them in that wilderness than the British and Americans combined. Nevertheless, the outbreak of war tended to cause more confusion and division among the Indians, instead of uniting them in a concerted course of action. Tribes often were split over what stance to take: pro-British, pro-American, or neutral. Different villages of the same tribe, or even individuals within the same village, sometimes supported opposite sides in the conflict. Many Indians fluctuated in their sentiments. Even among those who took an active part in the fighting, enthusiasm waxed and waned, and participation often was relatively brief. Foremost in the minds of the Indians was the desire to emerge on the winning side. British and American efforts to gain and retain the Indians' allegiance depended heavily on supplying them with gifts and trade goods.[26]

Although some tribes, or segments of tribes, remained neutral for a time, the majority of Indians sooner or later sided with the British, whom they considered less of a threat to their way of life than the Americans. The British also seemed better able to supply them with necessary trade items. Not surprisingly, many warriors viewed this conflict between England and the colonies as a great opportunity to drive back the frontier people. They were aided by the large amount of military supplies made available by the same British Army which many of them had been fighting just a few years earlier. In addition, the Indians often were joined in their raids and campaigns by British officers and soldiers, as well as by Americans still loyal to the crown.[27]

Richard White, in *The Middle Ground: Indians, Empires, and Republics in the Great Lakes Region, 1650-1815,* notes that those Indians who were the most effective in fighting were governed by their own determination to halt the frontiersmen's advance rather than by a strong fidelity to the British. Others who had lost relatives to the pioneers also fought bitterly and well. Most warriors without such motivations took a less active role.[28]

As in the case of the Indians, not all frontier people were united in their allegiances. Certain areas in particular were in turmoil, as some Americans supported the Revolutionary cause and others remained loyal to the British. For example, east of the Appalachian Mountains in the backcountry of South Carolina, whole neighborhoods were predominantly Patriot or Loyalist (also known as Tory). In many cases the choice was influenced by the views of the local men of prominence. The hunting pioneers in this region were bitter over years of harassment by colonial authorities, which caused many of these backwoodsmen to side with the British.[29]

West of the Appalachian Mountains in the Kentucky and Tennessee country, sentiments also were divided, particularly at the beginning of the Revolutionary War. These divisions usually were overcome quickly, however, by the necessity to mount a common defense against British-sponsored Indian attacks. In this vast wilderness region, the Indians posed more of a threat than they did back east of the Appalachians. In most cases, individuals with Loyalist leanings (a minority) were forced to join with those in favor of the Revolution in order to survive; raiding Indians did not take time to differentiate between Patriot and Loyalist families.[30]

The hunting pioneers and farming pioneers concentrated in small forts or stations where they took part in collective domestic and military efforts. (The words "fort" and "station" seem to have been used without any strict distinction between the two.) In some cases, the forts were built so that the cabins were completely within, and separate from, the stockade walls, which sometimes had bastions on the corners. In another common configuration, the dwellings were laid out facing a shared open area; then stockade walls were constructed to join the windowless rear walls of the cabins, linking them together to form one seamless perimeter. Regardless of the fort's layout, a heavy, barred gate completed the defenses.[31]

In some areas, hunting pioneers and farming pioneers were forced to spend several years forted-up. Though men often ranged widely outside these forts in hunting and military activities, women and children usually did not go much beyond the crop fields which were adjacent to the settlement. Any slaves present at a fort normally were restricted to its environs also, although they sometimes were sent to perform potentially dangerous chores.[32]

After his first disastrous attempt to settle in the Kentucky country in 1773, Daniel Boone successfully led a second group into the region in March 1775, just a month prior to the outbreak of the Revolutionary War. Operating under the auspices of a North Carolina land speculator, Boone established the fortified settlement of Boonesborough in central Kentucky. Other similar settlements were established in that region during this period. In July 1776, Boone's daughter, Jemima, and two other girls also in their teens, were captured near the fort by a small Shawnee and Cherokee raiding party and hurried north toward the Ohio River. Gathering several men, Boone started in pursuit. In a daring rescue, the captives were recovered three days later. The girls, weary from their passage through rough country, were otherwise unharmed.[33]

At the same time, 150 miles to the southeast, the Cherokee had decided to drive out the pioneers from the Watauga and Holston areas of what is now extreme northeastern Tennessee. Having learned of the Cherokee plans, the frontier people quickly gathered in forts. Eaton's Fort, at the Long Island of the Holston River, was on the route of the advancing Indian war party. Not wanting to give the warriors an opportunity to wreak havoc on the cabins and crops which had been hastily abandoned, approximately 170 militia marched out into the wilderness on July 20, 1776, to meet the Indians. The group was led by several captains; no one person was in charge. Because this area was on the edge of the frontier, it is likely that a considerable number of these men were hunting pioneers. About six miles from the fort, the advance scouts (or spies) encountered a forward party of Indians and fired on them. Both sides broke off this initial engagement, with the warriors in retreat.[34]

Now the element of surprise was gone and, after some discussion and disagreement, the frontiersmen began heading back toward the fort. Learning of this move, the whole Indian force rushed on, forgetting for a moment their customary caution. The pioneers had gone only a short distance when the main party of Indians caught up with them. Quickly forming a line which eventually extended through the woods about a quarter of a mile, and taking possession of a hill, the frontiersmen were able to prevent the warriors from surrounding them or gaining an advantageous position. Both sides appear to have been approximately equal in number. In the fierce struggle which followed, Chief Dragging Canoe, the main Indian leader, was wounded seriously. After another chief was killed in hand-to-hand combat, the Cherokee broke off the action. The official report of the battle, signed by six of the officers, relates that thirteen dead Indians had been found, and it was believed that many more had been killed. No frontiersmen were killed, although four men received severe wounds. "Never did troops fight with greater calmness than ours did. The Indians attacked us with the greatest fury imaginable, and made the most vigorous effort to surround us. Our spies really deserved the greatest applause."[35]

By 1777, full-scale war had engulfed the frontier. In the Kentucky country, less than three hundred hunting pioneers and farming pioneers in fortified settlements held out against increasing Indian raids from north of the Ohio River. These attacks made it extremely difficult for the frontier people to tend their fields or their animals. Most of the crops and livestock were destroyed by the Indians. As a result, the pioneers were to a large extent dependent on the skills of their best hunters. With Indian war parties lurking in the forest, hunting itself became an extremely dangerous activity, as the hunter suddenly could find himself the prey. Hunters would leave the fort before daylight, travel many miles, shoot a deer, and often return to the fort with the venison after dark.[36]

In September 1778, four hundred Shawnee warriors, led by Chief Blackfish and Chief Moluntha, arrived at Boonesborough determined to take the fort. Boone, who earlier that year had been taken captive by the Shawnee and then adopted before escaping, was present. The Indians tried to talk the fort's leaders, including their erstwhile adoptee, into surrendering. There followed several days of discussions while the Kentuckians played for time, hoping for the arrival of reinforcements which had been requested from Virginia. Finally, the warriors grew exasperated, and they attempted to capture the fort's leaders during the final parley. When that effort failed, the siege began in earnest.[37]

The long days which followed saw determined assaults, as well as attempts to set fire to the fort. Torches were made of loose hickory bark, cloth, and gunpowder, all tied around a stick eighteen to twenty-four inches in length. Indians approached as closely as possible in order to throw these firebrands over the walls and onto a cabin roof, an extremely hazardous undertaking which could prove fatal to the warriors. Smaller amounts of flaming material were attached to arrows which then were fired into the fort. A tunneling operation was tried, but it eventually was halted by a cave-in. Tunneling toward a besieged fort was done in an effort to gain underground entry, to undermine the log posts, or to place explosive charges under the walls; it was a tactic used only rarely by Indians.[38]

During this Revolutionary War era, attempts to capture forts such as Boonesborough usually failed. Part of the reason may have been the frontiersmen's highly accurate marksmanship using the recently acquired long rifle. The defenders normally could prevent the warriors from getting close enough to the stockade walls to set them on fire or scale them. In addition, fires which were started by flaming arrows or tossed firebrands ordinarily could be extinguished before critical damage was done. The uncommon tenacity of the Indians in the confrontation at Boonesborough is indicated by Boone's estimate of thirty-seven warriors killed during the week of fighting. Casualties within the fort were two people killed and four wounded.[39]

In the meantime, a particularly dynamic and resourceful military leader was emerging out of the struggle on the frontier, an officer destined to exceed all others in his influence on the American Revolution west of the Appalachians. George Rogers Clark, a major of militia in Kentucky, was the ideal backwoods commander. Raised as a member of the Virginia gentry and exhibiting the confident bearing which that background would instill, he had demonstrated bravery and wilderness skills during his years on the frontier. He also possessed an aptitude for direct and stirring action which inspired and animated his followers.

In an effort to curb Indian attacks from north of the

Ohio River, Clark devised a plan for an army to be led into that British-controlled region to capture the old French settlements which furnished the warriors with supplies. Most of the French in this region had been resigned to, but not enthusiastic about, living under the British rule instituted following France's defeat in the French and Indian War. Clark hoped that with the appearance of an American force in the area these French settlers could be won to the Patriot side. In 1777, two men whom Clark had sent as spies to the western Illinois country returned with current information on conditions in the French settlements there. They had succeeded in their mission by posing as hunters and by keeping their Patriot sentiments hidden from authorities.[40]

Early in 1778, Clark's plans were approved by Virginia, which, in addition to the western Pennsylvania region, also claimed the Kentucky country. Promoted to lieutenant-colonel (and later colonel and brigadier-general), Clark enlisted 150 backwoodsmen primarily from northwestern Virginia and southwestern Pennsylvania. Moving down the Ohio River in May and June of 1778, they were joined by a small number of frontiersmen from what is now northeastern Tennessee and central Kentucky, bringing to approximately 175 the total strength of Clark's command. Considering the areas from which this small army was recruited, it is likely that hunting pioneers were well represented.[41]

While enroute down the Ohio River, Clark's force encountered a party of American hunters who had been in the Illinois country despite the war. More importantly, they had visited British-governed Kaskaskia, the French settlement which was Clark's immediate objective. Now declaring their sympathy with the Patriot cause, the hunters provided important information and asked permission to join the expedition. Guided by one of these men, Clark's force abandoned their boats and marched overland from the Ohio River through the wilderness of the southern Illinois country. Encountering no one enroute, the frontiersmen achieved complete surprise and captured Kaskaskia on July 4, 1778. Winning the French inhabitants to the American cause with surprising ease, Clark quickly extended his control to the nearby settlement of Cahokia and then to Vincennes, which is located on the Wabash River in present-day southwestern Indiana. In addition, during several weeks in August and September, Clark held discussions with many of the tribes in the region. Although his small army was greatly outnumbered by these assembled warriors, Clark used a combination of bravado and threats, intermixed with more conciliatory remarks, to gain their acceptance of his arrival in the Illinois country. As a result, during the next few critical months most of these particular Indians would favor the Americans or take a neutral stance.[42]

Learning of Clark's success north of the Ohio River, British Lieutenant-Governor Henry Hamilton departed from Detroit in October. His force consisted of British redcoats and local Indian allies, plus militia drawn from Detroit's primarily French population. On his way to Fort Sackville in Vincennes, Hamilton gathered additional Indians still loyal to the British, bringing his total array to 500 men. The American officer whom Clark had placed in command at the Wabash River post was captured, and the French inhabitants were required to renew their pledge of fealty to the British. Instead of continuing on to confront Clark in the Illinois country, however, Hamilton made two serious mistakes; he allowed the Indians to leave, and he sent part of his French contingent back home to Detroit for the winter. He planned to gather his forces again in the spring and then move against Clark.[43]

Informed of the situation at Vincennes, Clark decided

to take the immediate offensive. In a bold move, he set out from Kaskaskia in early February 1779. His force consisted of less than a hundred hunting pioneers and farming pioneers remaining from his original command, augmented by new French recruits, bringing his total army back up to approximately 175 men. In making the epic, eighteen-day, midwinter trek across the Illinois wilds, Clark's men found it necessary to wade for extended periods through icy waters, sometimes shoulder deep. The incredible wilderness hardships which they encountered would have deterred or killed less hardy individuals. With the British believing themselves safe from any attack during this season, the Americans achieved complete surprise when they arrived at Vincennes after dark on February 23. They were greeted eagerly by the French inhabitants who lived in dwellings near the fort.[44]

Inside the fort, Hamilton's garrison consisted of approximately forty British regular troops along with about the same number of Detroit militia, who were mostly French. Taking up protected positions around the stockade walls, Clark's men opened fire; some Vincennes French also joined them. Many of the frontiersmen were within twenty or thirty yards of the fort in a location below the trajectory of its cannons. The riflemen's accurate fire subjected the defenders to imminent peril every time the fort's gunports were opened. Several of the British soldiers were hit. In the dark, musket fire from the fort was ineffective against attackers who were utilizing the cover of buildings, fence palings, trenches, breastworks, and the bank of the nearby Wabash River.[45]

Part of Clark's strategy was to convince Hamilton through a great deal of activity and noise that the fort was being threatened by a much larger army than actually existed. During the night, the besieging force alternated periods of scattered shooting with shorter intervals of concentrated gunfire aimed from all directions. At times, fifty frontiersmen who were in reserve in the town purposefully made as much noise as possible by yelling and loudly laughing. Also, work appeared to be starting behind the riverbank about thirty feet from the stockade walls; this operation was intended to suggest that men were busily engaged in tunneling operations. All of these tactics were meant to give the impression that although there were many frontiersmen on the firing line, they were but a relatively small portion of those available. Before the arrival of daylight could render the riflemen more vulnerable, and also reveal their true numbers, they withdrew to more protected positions further from the fort.[46]

The diverse actions of the attacking army served to intimidate the defenders and at the same time convinced Hamilton that Clark had arrived with formidable military strength. In addition, with the local French outside the fort once more clearly supporting Clark, Hamilton no longer could be certain of the loyalty of the Detroit French who were inside the fort. Further heightening the pressure on Hamilton, Clark peremptorily called on the British to surrender. He then let it be known in discussions regarding capitulation that his men would give no quarter if ultimately forced to storm the fort.[47]

That Clark's statement was not an idle threat soon was illustrated graphically. During a lull in the fighting, a war party of approximately twenty Indians who were returning with scalps from a raid on the Kentucky frontier unwittingly walked into the American lines. Realizing too late their mistake, most of the warriors were killed or captured. In retribution for the ongoing killing of frontier people, the backwoodsmen tomahawked the captured warriors in front of the fort. This grim episode, characteristic of the harsh realities of frontier warfare, was meant to serve also as an object lesson for the watching British. Shortly thereafter, Hamilton agreed to Clark's final terms of surrender.[48]

Following the retaking of Fort Sackville, Clark next turned his attention to capturing British-held Detroit. He was informed that five hundred reinforcements to his small command would be sent by Virginia. In addition, Colonel John Bowman was expected to bring three hundred men from the Kentucky country, where the population and the number of fortified stations had been increasing rapidly as a result of Clark's success north of the Ohio River the previous year. However, the contingent which was sent by Virginia turned out to be only 150 frontiersmen, and Bowman decided to lead his Kentucky force first against the Shawnee village of Chillicothe.[49]

Bowman's expedition was destined to be just one of several major wilderness campaigns against the Indian towns in the Ohio country during the coming years. In these expeditions, certain common elements usually were present. Although the men sometimes rode horses enroute to their destination, they did most of their fighting while dismounted. The general lack of pistols and swords, as well as the nature and terrain of the battle sites, tended to reduce the effectiveness of mounted warfare; even so, on occasion a charge on horseback could be decisive. When attacking Indian settlements, an army's first objective was surprise, which would enable the frontiersmen to surround the village, cut off any escape, and then defeat the warriors. Whether or not this goal was achieved totally, the next objective would be to destroy the village and any food supplies (either standing crops or caches) which were not appropriated for the campaign; the destruction of food often compelled the Indians to spend their time during the coming months hunting rather than raiding. Another aim was to take Indian captives, usually women and children who were less able to flee in the confusion of an attack. These prisoners later could be exchanged for captives taken by the Indians. Finally, there always was the intention of seizing as much plunder as possible, including horses, weapons, and furs. Often, these spoils of war were auctioned off to the frontiersmen, and then the proceeds would be divided equally among them.

Setting out in May 1779, Bowman and three hundred hunting pioneers and farming pioneers reached Chillicothe undetected under the cover of darkness. Bowman divided his command in order to surround the Shawnee town. As daylight appeared, the fighting commenced. A number of warriors took refuge in a fortified council house from which they directed a deadly fire on the frontiersmen. A general retreat began with the Indians soon following in pursuit, and a running battle ensued. The frontiersmen turned about to make stands against their pursuers; eventually a determined charge by the Kentucky force succeeded in dispersing the Indians and ending the pursuit. Nine pioneers were killed on this expedition; Indian losses are unknown, but they included Red Hawk, one of their leaders. Much of the town and crops had been destroyed and a large number of horses and other spoils appropriated. After returning to Kentucky, the majority of these frontiersmen concluded that they had experienced enough fighting for a time. As a result, instead of the expected three hundred reinforcements from Kentucky, only thirty men joined Clark and his small force in Vincennes for the anticipated campaign against the British post of Detroit. Not having received the expected amount of aid from either Virginia or Kentucky, Clark was obliged to abandon his plan to capture Detroit.[50]

A year later, in 1780, British-led Indians captured two small forts in Kentucky after threatening to fire on them with cannons. Determined to retaliate for this latest incursion, Clark decided to move north from Kentucky against the Shawnee towns from which many of the attackers had been gathered. This was the same area in the Ohio country which Bowman had marched against a year earlier. Boone, who had been on a visit to his relatives in North Carolina at the time of Bowman's raid, would serve as an officer on this campaign. It is likely that a significant portion of the frontiersmen mobilized for this expedition were hunting pioneers, although persons interested primarily in land speculation or farming were coming to Kentucky in rapidly growing numbers. In order to recruit some of the more avid landseekers, Clark even found it necessary to close down the land offices temporarily.[51]

Crossing the Ohio River with a thousand men in early August 1780, Clark led the Americans northward to chastise the enemy. They took along a cannon to batter down any defenses such as had stymied Bowman's men at the council house. Learning of the army's approach, the Shawnee in recently rebuilt Chillicothe set fire to the town and retreated to the neighboring settlement of Piqua. After feasting on Shawnee corn and completing the destruction of Chillicothe and most of its agricultural fields, Clark's force moved on to Piqua.[52]

Although outnumbered, the Indians were waiting and opened fire on the advancing Americans. Taking advantage of available cover, both the warriors and the frontiersmen extended their lines in an effort to outflank their opponents. The Americans gradually gained the advantage, and the Indians were driven back through the tall grass and trees to their fortifications, which included a blockhouse. Now the cannon proved its worth, as the warriors were forced out of their stronghold by the destructive round shot. The Indians attempted an attack but were repulsed; they then withdrew and abandoned the town.[53]

The fighting had lasted approximately three hours. Complete success eluded the Americans, because a contingent of men whom Clark had sent to encircle the town and cut off any escape had been delayed by the difficult terrain. More than twenty frontiersmen were listed as killed or seriously wounded in the battle; Indian losses are more difficult to ascertain, but they probably were comparable. The Shawnee now fully realized that their villages north of the Ohio River offered them no sanctuary from retaliatory attacks. In addition, the destruction of their towns and crops caused them great hardship during the following winter.[54]

Unlike the other confrontations described in this chapter, the Battle of King's Mountain in October 1780 was fought between Patriots and Loyalists only. No Indians were involved. During the Revolution, the backcountry of the Carolinas east of the Appalachians was the scene of bitter warfare between those Americans seeking independence and other Americans still loyal to the crown. There, as mentioned previously, the Loyalist ranks included some hunting pioneers. At the same time, a number of hunting pioneers and farming pioneers, known as "over-mountain men" (because they had moved west of the Appalachians), had traveled back east of the mountains to assist the local Patriots. The fighting, much of it among former friends and neighbors, grew increasingly bitter. Frequently no quarter was given. As part of his overall strategy to subdue the southern states, Lord Charles Cornwallis had detached British Major Patrick Ferguson from his main army and sent him inland with a small contingent of Tory troops brought from the north; their mission was to gather and reinforce the Loyalists in the Carolina backcountry. Ferguson's activities only served to increase the level of animosity and warfare between the local Tories and Patriots.[55]

In August 1780, a major American army was defeated by Cornwallis' British troops at the Battle of Camden in central South Carolina. After this crushing loss, the Patriots were greatly disheartened. Most of the over-mountain men operating in the Carolina backcountry withdrew for a time to their homes west of the Appalachian Mountains. Ferguson and his Loyalists trailed them to the eastern edge of the mountains, carrying out reprisals against Patriot families along the way. Ferguson then made the mistake of sending a message to the over-mountain men threatening to cross the mountains, lay waste their country, and hang their leaders. Viewing this taunt as an insult and a challenge, and already being disposed to sally forth again out of their strongholds, a large force of hunting pioneers and farming pioneers gathered west of the mountains in September 1780.[56]

Determined to take vengeance on Ferguson and the Loyalists in his command, the over-mountain men crossed the Appalachians and descended the eastern side. Proceeding onward, they gathered additional men; the army as finally composed included contingents from Virginia, North Carolina, South Carolina, Georgia, and present-day Tennessee. Learning of this development, Ferguson, now somewhat alarmed, began to retreat east toward Cornwallis' main army at Charlotte, North Carolina. Fearing that the Tories would escape, those Patriots who were mounted on the swiftest horses pressed on. In the meantime, Ferguson had decided to make a stand at King's Mountain, thirty-five miles short of Charlotte. In coming to this fateful decision, he probably was driven by a sense of pride, a desire for military glory, and a low regard for what he referred to as his "backwater barbarian" adversaries. King's Mountain, near the border between present-day North Carolina and South Carolina, was not as impressive in appearance as its name might imply. A long ridge rising a relatively short distance from the surrounding terrain, it had steep and wooded sides, but the flat top was largely devoid of trees. There, on a surface several hundred yards long and less than half as wide, Ferguson drew up his army of approximately one thousand men to await the arrival of his opponents.[57]

The pursuing Patriot force had fluctuated widely in numbers during the expedition eastward, but now it was roughly comparable in size to that of Ferguson's command. The pursuers were led by their principal field-grade officers: William Campbell, John Sevier, Isaac Shelby, Charles McDowell, and Benjamin Cleveland. Dividing their army to surround the mountain, they began moving up the slopes. The ensuing hour-long battle would pit the European-style tactics in which Ferguson had drilled his Tories (including any hunting pioneers in his ranks) against the typical backwoods fighting style of the frontiersmen.[58]

Taking aim from the forested cover of the slopes, the first Patriots to reach the summit poured in an accurate fire. Ferguson directed a portion of his men, arrayed in the open, to advance using regular or makeshift bayonets to close with their enemies. Imitating Indian wilderness tactics, the Patriots melted down the slopes into the wooded cover, keeping the Tories from effectively pressing their attack. As Ferguson's men moved back to the flat summit, they were followed by the rallying Patriots who fired on them. In addition, the Tories soon were coming under fire from their adversaries on other sides of the mountain. Further bayonet charges by the Tories at different points on the mountain only produced the same results as the first: the Patriots retreated down the slopes, rallied, and followed their opponents back to the summit, firing as they went. Eventually the Patriots were firing from all sides, killing and wounding a mounting number of Ferguson's men. Ferguson was cut down, riddled with several rifle balls. Seeing their leader killed, the Tories surrendered. Because the victors were so caught up in the fighting, and their animosity was so great, they continued to fire on the Loyalists for a time.[59]

Although estimates of casualties in Ferguson's army vary, it appears that the Tories suffered over three hundred killed or wounded; Patriot losses totaled less than a hundred. Approximately seven hundred of Ferguson's men were taken prisoner. Resentment continued to run high among the victors, particularly against those who were believed to have committed previous outrages. Subsequently, more than thirty of the Tories were found guilty and condemned to death by a hastily assembled court composed of several officers. Nine of Ferguson's men had been hanged, when suddenly the Patriot leaders decided to pardon the remainder who stood nearby awaiting their fate.[60]

The American victory over the British at Yorktown, Virginia, the following year in 1781 largely ended warfare in the East. By contrast, on the frontier the struggle against the British and Indians continued unabated in many areas, including the rugged and wooded terrain of western Pennsylvania and the eastern Ohio country. Hunting pioneers and farming pioneers from the Fort Pitt region had begun migrating into the eastern Ohio country in the mid-1770s, coincident with the start of the Revolutionary War. There they tended to settle in groups for mutual protection. The continuing warfare in this whole upper Ohio River region caused the frontier people to become increasingly hostile toward all Indians. This animosity extended even to the peaceful Moravian mission Indians in the Ohio country, who were wrongly suspected of helping raiding warriors. These bitter feelings led to the brutal execution of almost a hundred of these Indians, including women and children, by a group of frontiersmen in March 1782. Shortly after this massacre, backwoodsmen in the Fort Pitt region decided to launch an attack on the important Wyandot villages on the Sandusky River in the northwestern Ohio country.[61]

Strategically located within easy traveling distance of the British headquarters at Detroit, the Wyandot towns were a major supply depot and staging point for raids; other British-allied tribes, the Shawnee, Mingo, and Delaware, were not far distant. Four hundred and eighty frontiersmen, both hunting pioneers and farming pioneers, volunteered for the campaign. Included in this number were individuals who had participated in the killing of the Moravian Indians. Under the command of Colonel William Crawford, the army set out on horseback late in May 1782 and made its way through more than 150 miles of Ohio country wilderness. The force emerged from the deep woods at the Sandusky Plains near the Wyandot towns on June 3. Because the plans for the expedition had become known to the Indians, the Wyandot were in the process of being reinforced by Shawnee, Mingo, and Delaware warriors, the latter being kinsmen of the executed mission Indians.[62]

On June 4, action commenced with Crawford's force securing possession of a grove of trees after a brief skirmish with the Indians. The warriors then quickly surrounded the grove. Heavy firing continued for several hours until nightfall, as the Indians were held at bay. Both sides remained largely in place during the following day while engaged in sporadic, long-range firing. This relative inaction proved a costly mistake for the pioneers, because Indian reinforcements continued to arrive. The warriors also had been joined by Tory rangers from Detroit. This formidable Indian and Tory array as finally assembled was headed by British Captain William Caldwell and several chiefs, including The Pipe, Wingenund, and Zhausshotoh. Realizing they were in an increasingly precarious position, the frontiersmen determined that a retreat under cover of night was necessary.[63]

Trying to break out of their encirclement, Crawford's men were disoriented by the darkness and by the harassment from Indians who were encountered on the way. As a result, many of them became lost and separated. Some of the men were forced to abandon horses which had become mired in swamps and bogs. The next day, the majority of the frontiersmen were able to regroup and continue their retreat, with the Indians and their Tory allies soon in full pursuit. The pioneers eventually made a stand and in a sharp action drove the enemy back. As the retreat of the frontiersmen again commenced, the Indians and Tories harried them by firing from a distance. The next morning the pursuit finally ended approximately forty miles from where the original fighting had taken place three days earlier. From that point, the pioneers were able to continue unmolested in their return to the upper Ohio River area. Survivors of this campaign continued to straggle in for some time after the main body of men had returned. For this reason, estimates of the total number of frontiersmen killed varied from thirty to seventy. Indian and Tory losses undoubtedly were less.[64]

Crawford and several others were captured in the confusion of the retreat. Their subsequent treatment may have been due in part to the warriors' desire to avenge the execution of the mission Indians. Some of the captives were tomahawked. Others were slated to be burned to death. Although Crawford had not participated in the massacre, he nevertheless was burned at the stake, an occurrence which became widely known on the frontier.[65]

Following the defeat of Crawford's army in the Ohio country, Captain William Caldwell led a war party composed of three hundred Indians and fifty Tory rangers from north of the Ohio River against the frontier of central Kentucky. After traveling through the wilderness, they laid siege to Bryan's Station on the morning of August 16, 1782. The inhabitants managed to send a message requesting aid, and reinforcements soon arrived to help defend the fort. As the Indians retreated north, a force of 180 mounted frontiersmen, undoubtedly including a significant number of hunting pioneers, quickly gathered under the leadership of their field-grade officers John Todd, Stephen Trigg, and Daniel Boone. It was decided to begin pursuit without waiting for additional contingents.[66]

While following the enemy through the woods, Boone soon noted that the Indians and Tories were making no effort to conceal their route. It appeared, however, that they were trying to hide their true numbers by treading in each other's footsteps. Arriving at the Licking River near the Blue Licks in northern Kentucky on August 19, Boone warned his fellow frontiersmen that it would be dangerous to cross at that point. He believed their foes were waiting in ambush in the rough terrain on the other side. Most of the officers agreed with Boone, but the hotheaded Major Hugh McGary called on those who were not cowards to follow him in an immediate advance across the river. This challenge ended all rational discussion, and soon the entire command was on the other side.[67]

Leaving most of the horses at the river's edge, the frontiersmen advanced inland. Suddenly their enemies fired from cover, killing many of the Kentuckians in the first volley. Overwhelmed by the onslaught, the pioneers retreated, at times engaging with the enemy in hand-to-hand fighting. In this wild battle which continued as they recrossed the river, the outnumbered frontiersmen took heavy losses. Approximately seventy of the Kentuckians were killed, including some who were tortured to death. Among the dead were Todd, Trigg, and Boone's son, Israel. Ironically, McGary survived. Indian and Tory losses are uncertain, but undoubtedly they were considerably less.[68]

In response to this crushing defeat, George Rogers Clark again recruited a force of over a thousand men and led them across the Ohio River toward the Shawnee villages in early November 1782. Certainly many among them were hunting pioneers. Boone was one of the officers. Moving north through the deep forests, the frontiersmen managed to surprise the Indians at their main town of Piqua, quickly capturing it as the inhabitants fled. Clark immediately sent out detachments to destroy nearby Indian towns and food supplies; Boone led one of these raids. The high point of the campaign was the looting and destruction of a major trading post which had supplied the Indians with British goods. Clark remained in the area several days, but he was not able to bring the enemy to battle. Instead, the frontiersmen had to content themselves with occasional long-range skirmishing. Clark's army had suffered only a few casualties; Indian losses were somewhat larger. A number of Indian captives also were taken.[69]

Following the official conclusion of the Revolutionary War in 1783, raids by the tribes continued. Although Clark had resigned his commission as a brigadier-general, in 1786 the militia leaders in Kentucky asked him to accept command of a force to retaliate against the Indians north of the Ohio River. Again, hunting pioneers would be among those taking part. Despite misgivings regarding his legal authority, Clark set off in mid-September with an unruly array of more than a thousand men, this time intending to march up the banks of the Wabash River to attack Miami and Kickapoo villages in that area. The refusal of some of the men to proceed eventually compelled him to turn back before arriving at his objective.[70]

Before Clark had started out, it had been decided that hunting pioneers and farming pioneers still being gathered would join a second force under Colonel Benjamin Logan to attack the Shawnee towns in the Ohio country. Setting out with about eight hundred frontiersmen, including Daniel Boone, Logan crossed the Ohio River in late September. Many of the

Shawnee had left to support the other Indians waiting to confront Clark on the Wabash River to the west. As a result, Logan's men were largely unopposed when their wilderness trek ended at the Shawnee villages. Among the warriors killed in the brief fighting was one who had participated in 1773 in the torture and death of Boone's son, James, during Boone's failed first attempt to settle in Kentucky. After an important chief surrendered to the frontiersmen, he was tomahawked by Hugh McGary, much to the consternation of the other officers. The Americans destroyed several villages along with large caches of corn and then returned to Kentucky. Losses on both sides were relatively light. A considerable number of prisoners, mostly women and children, were taken. This was Boone's last major campaign.[71]

Thus, we come to the end of some examples of warfare in which the hunting pioneers, as well as other frontiersmen, were involved. These Revolutionary War era battles constituted the most intense period of fighting ever participated in by both hunting pioneers and farming pioneers. After 1786, soldiers of the new United States Army increasingly would dominate the major campaigns on the frontier. Nevertheless, frontiersmen would continue to take part in these actions as militia auxiliaries, playing a particularly important role in the War of 1812. Although their performances varied considerably from battle to battle throughout the years, the majority of both the hunting pioneers and the farming pioneers proved themselves daring, courageous, and capable in the exceedingly grim activity of wilderness warfare.

4

THE OHIO RIVER VALLEY

Following the Revolutionary War, there was a great influx of hunting pioneers and farming pioneers into both the eastern Ohio country and the Kentucky region. This movement into the Trans-Appalachian wilderness occurred despite continuing Indian attacks, which generally took the form of small-scale raids. These sporadic assaults often proved fatal to the frontier people; hundreds of individuals were killed during this period.

In the Kentucky region, where no federal surveying of lands was being conducted as a prelude to legal settlement, the "land fever" had reached new heights under a chaotic system of acquisition. Even some hunting pioneers, including Daniel Boone, were not immune to this opportunity to gain legal possession of land. Boone soon was filing claims on thousands of acres in the Kentucky country. Utilizing his vast knowledge of this region, he was able to achieve initial success in surveying land and filing claims for himself and others. At this time, Boone also entered into new occupations which definitely were not typical of the hunting pioneers, including sheriff, legislator, innkeeper, and proprietor of a general merchandise business. Unlike the great majority of those who were, or had been, hunting pioneers, Boone owned slaves during this period.[1]

Despite all his activities, Boone soon found himself in increasingly difficult financial straits. The root of his problem was Kentucky's land system, which was fueled by the frenetic activities of speculators and farming pioneers. Many of these individuals were much more skilled than Boone in the intricacies of legal requirements and paperwork. As a result, he became enmeshed in a welter of claims, counterclaims, and lawsuits. As the years went by, his other business ventures also failed to prosper. Boone would return then to the deep woods, again spending extended periods hunting in the sylvan wilds which still remained in the Kentucky country and in what is now West Virginia.[2]

It was during this post-Revolutionary War period, in 1783, that John Filson interviewed Boone while researching a book on Kentucky. Filson was impressed with the frontiersman, and when the writer's work was published in 1784 it was entitled *The Discovery, Settlement and Present State of Kentucke . . . To which is added An Appendix, Containing The Adventures of Col. Daniel Boon.* The book soon would make Boone famous in America and Europe. It was particularly popular in European intellectual and literary circles, where Boone came to be viewed as a philosopher of the woods.[3]

In 1794, at the Battle of Fallen Timbers near Lake Erie, General Anthony Wayne's force achieved a major victory over the northern tribes who had been raiding both north and south of the Ohio River. The resultant Treaty of Greenville the following year ended overt hostilities on the frontier for the next decade and a half. Subsequently, the floodgates of settlement were thrown open west of the Appalachians. Previously, the lifestyle of the hunting pioneers had been hampered by the Indian warriors with muskets and tomahawks. Now, their main concern would be farmers with axes and plows. Because of this threat from the farmers, the hunting pioneers dispersed out of those parts of the Ohio country and the newly established state of Kentucky which were becoming settled. For a time, some of these individuals gravitated to the uninhabited stretches along the Ohio River, where they thrived during the ensuing years of tranquillity.

This period of peace made possible a great increase in travel west of the Appalachians by Americans from the more settled East and by foreign visitors as well. Most of these travelers entered the West by floating down the Ohio River; sometimes they made excursions of varying distances inland. This type of itinerary afforded them numerous opportunities to view the hunting pioneers, just as these backwoods people were entering their optimum era of living in the wilderness. Many of these travelers continued the already well-established tradition of writing accounts of their journeys. The narratives from this period give us some of the best descriptions of the hunting pioneers and their way of life.

The new surge of travelers coincided with a growing interest within the European (and later American) intellectual, literary, and artistic communities regarding the glories of nature and wilderness. This enlivened attentiveness toward such natural themes would affect the writing of many of the travelers who described the hunting pioneers. Of particular significance is the contrast between this new, idealized concept of the natural world and the attitude of ambivalence previously associated with wilderness during much of the growth of Western Civilization. Two schools of thought were primarily responsible for bringing about this change in outlook: Deism and Romanticism.

Deism postulated that God could be known to exist only through reason and the natural world. Deists were impressed with the grandeur of wilderness, which inspired contemplation and awe. In that setting, God and spiritual truths could be discerned most easily.

Although influenced by Deism, Romanticists tended to place more emphasis on emotion and the senses. The Romanticists had a predilection for the remote, mysterious, uncultivated, unkempt, and primitive. Scenes of castle ruins in a wild, abandoned landscape or sublime views of pure, untrammeled wilderness were prominent in Romantic art and literary descriptions.

One of the most important eighteenth-century intellectuals associated with these schools of thought was Jean-Jacques Rousseau. Reflecting the Romanticist's emphasis on the primitive, he brought to the forefront and articulated the somewhat vague concept of the "noble savage" living in the wilderness. According to Rousseau, mankind's basic needs are best met when they live in a natural state; civilized life only brings unneeded problems. He believed that as long as people are satisfied in a simple and primitive existence, they are free, happy, and healthy. The development of unnatural and unnecessary wants only results in the destruction of their original ideal condition. Under this theory, it is the savage life which possesses real virtue.[4]

Far from the American frontier, European Romanticists held the common Old World view of Indians as a people living a simple and primitive hunting existence in the wilderness. Not surprisingly, the Native Americans were considered a perfect example of Rousseau's "noble savage." Some of this esteem for the Indians was extended later to the hunting pioneers, such as the then well-known Daniel Boone. These frontier people were seen by Romanticists as rejecting much of civilization in an effort to return to a more simple and primitive life. Some Americans living in the East, also far removed from the frontier, held this same Romantic view of the Indians and hunting pioneers as "noble savages" in the deep woods.

Clearly under the influence of Rousseau and other Romantic writers, English traveler Francis Baily wrote of his experiences in the upper Ohio River wilderness in his *Journal of a Tour in Unsettled Parts of North America in 1796 and 1797*. After their boat had become locked in the ice for the winter, Baily's party found their provisions running low. Taking turns going out with a gun each morning, they were totally dependent on the vagaries of the hunt for their food. According to Baily, even in these circumstances they found themselves happy. They enjoyed the great blessing of good health and were not concerned with all the artificial wants which afflict men in civilization. The procuring of food became one of their chief pleasures. It also provided great amusement and diversion. "Whether it were the novelty of the thing which attracted us, or the scenery of the country, and the sublimity of its views, so very different from what we had been used to in the old country, I know not; but certain it is, there is something so very attractive in a life spent in this manner, that were I disposed to become a hermit, and seclude myself from the world, the woods of America would be my retreat: there should I with my dog and my gun, and the hollow of a rock for my habitation, enjoy undisturbed all that fancied bliss attendant on a state of nature."[5]

Baily notes that while hunting he often became lost in contemplation due to the novelty and the grandeur of the scenery. "Happy men! cried I, who, ignorant of all the deceits and artifices attendant on a state of civilization, unpracticed in the vices and dissipation of degraded humanity, unconscious of artificial and unnecessary wants, secluded from all those pomps and ridiculous ostentations which serve to enslave one half of a nation for the gratification of the other; unshackled with the terrors which fanaticism and superstition inspire;

enjoying equally the free blessing which nature intended for man, how much, alas! how much I envy you!" Baily contends that if only he could renounce the habits which custom and education had given him, he cheerfully would join the backwoodsmen in their lifestyle, which included the three greatest blessings God can bestow: health, happiness, and independence. He ends these ruminations by concluding that the arts and sciences often do not bring the happiness man formerly enjoyed in a state of nature, and at the same time vices, misery, and oppression are glaringly evident in civilized society.[6]

After the spring thaw had released their boat from the ice of the upper Ohio River, Baily and his companions proceeded on their journey. Near present-day Cincinnati, a canoe containing a man and a dog came alongside. "We called to him to come into our boat, which he accordingly did; and after a little conversation our guest proved to be old Colonel Boon, the first discoverer of the now flourishing state of Kentucky." Baily had with him a copy of a geography book written by Gilbert Imlay which included Filson's narrative of Boone's life on the frontier. Delighted to be able to converse with the subject of the many adventures therein described, Baily read the account to Boone, and the latter confirmed its accuracy. When Baily came to the description of Boone's adventures with the Indians during the Revolutionary War, the frontiersman's face lit up, and he described events in minute detail.[7]

Baily asked Boone whether it gave him secret satisfaction to see a region which he had played a conspicuous part in discovering and settling change from wilderness to civilization. Boone, with a significant frown, stated that the people had gotten too proud, and then he spoke of the disadvantages of civilization. Baily understood his meaning, "and soon found that he was one of that class of men who, from nature and habit, was nearly allied in disposition and manners to an Indian," and "who form the first class of settlers in a country." Boone said he did not want to live where men "were shackled in their habits, and would not enjoy uncontrolled the free blessings which nature has bestowed upon them." He told Baily that he spent a great deal of time on the frontiers and was on his way to hunt for beaver in some remote area of the forest, where undisturbed he could "enjoy the pleasures arising from a secluded and solitary life." Shortly after this meeting with Baily on the Ohio River, Boone moved permanently westward with his family to the Missouri country across the Mississippi River.[8]

Georges Henri Victor Collot was a high-ranking French military officer who traveled through the Trans-Appalachian region in 1796. His book entitled *A Journey in North America* provides insight into the lives of the hunting pioneers: "The first class called *Forest Men*, holds the first line on the side of the Indian nations; these, properly speaking are Nomades, who do not cultivate lands, and who have no other employment than hunting, making excursions into the woods, and trafficking with the Indians: they often pass whole years amidst deserts, and have no fixed abode: a hut, covered with the bark of trees, and supported by two poles; a large fire placed on the side of the opening; a great blanket in which they wrap themselves up when they sleep, placing their feet towards the fire and their head in the cabin; these are all that is necessary to shelter them from the inclemency of the weather, and to pass the longest and severest nights." These "Forest Men" or hunting pioneers stay in an area until it becomes more populated and the game diminishes, and then they move forty or fifty miles further into the wilds, to find what they consider better living and more freedom.[9]

The next class which Collot describes is what he terms the "First Settlers," who are in some respects similar to the "Forest Men" but are "more fixed, depend less on hunting for subsistence," clear some land, and raise some cattle and hogs. They build fortified log dwellings to withstand Indian attacks. In these encounters, "the American defends himself with courage; his wife does not hesitate to take a musket, and, placed by his side at one of the crannies, fires on the invader; the children also take part in the engagement." These "First Settlers" generally remain four or five years until the population in the area becomes too large. Then they sell their improvements (not the land itself, which they do not own) to the "Great Settlers," whom Collot calls the "real husbandmen" and the "good farmers."[10]

Traveling down the Ohio River, Collot comments on a thirty-mile stretch which was uninhabited except for "a few huts belonging to hunters." Arriving at Red Banks on the Kentucky side of the river downstream from Louisville, he writes, "The inhabitants of Red Banks are only hunters, or what are called foresters." They raise no crops, but subsist by hunting and fishing. "At our arrival, we found a number of these hunters who had assembled to regale themselves on the banks of the river with the spoils of their chase on the preceding day, when they had killed a very fine buffaloe. They had drunk plentifully of whisky, and though the greater number were intoxicated, they were amusing themselves in firing with carabines against a piece of plank tied to a tree, which is called shooting at a mark." Collot was greatly impressed with their skill and accuracy, all the more so in view of their lack of sobriety.[11]

Continuing downriver, Collot arrived at the famous landmark on the Illinois side known as Big Cave or Cave-in-Rock. There he and his party observed several bears cooling off in the water. One of the bears suddenly decided to cross the river, and Collot with two French-Canadian boatmen and a hunter launched a small canoe and started in pursuit. Collot relates that bears "are often seen, even in broad day, swimming across the largest rivers, and it is while they are on their passage that the hunters attack them." The bear soon noticed them and tried to outdistance their canoe by swimming downstream with the current. After a half-hour of hard paddling, the men overtook the bear and began firing; it survived six hits before finally being finished off with an ax.[12]

Francois Andre Michaux's *Travels to the West of the Alleghany Mountains in the States of Ohio, Kentucky, and Tennessee* gives that Frenchman's observations of the hunting pioneers in 1802: "The inhabitants on the borders of the Ohio, employ the greatest part of their time in stag and bear hunting, for the sake of the skins, which they dispose of. The taste that they have contracted for this kind of life is prejudicial to the culture of their lands; besides they have scarcely any time to meliorate their new possessions, that usually consist of two or three hundred acres, of which not more than eight or ten are cleared. Nevertheless, the produce that they derive from them, with the milk of their cows, is sufficient for themselves and families, which are always very numerous." Corn is the only crop raised. The "miserable log houses, without windows," which they occupy are in contrast to the beauties of their riverfront locations. These hunting pioneers are hospitable to travelers, allowing them to sleep on the floor in their dwellings and providing them with a meal.[13]

"More than half of those who inhabit the borders of the Ohio, are again the first inhabitants, or as they are called in the United States, the first settlers, a kind of men who cannot settle upon the soil that they have cleared, and who under pretence of finding a better land, a more wholesome country, a greater abundance of game, push forward, incline perpetually towards the most distant points of the American population, go and settle in the neighborhood of the savage nations, whom they brave even in their own country." Michaux states that the behavior of these people toward the Indians brings on frequent conflict in which the hunting pioneers often fall victim. This is because they are outnumbered, not because they lack courage.[14]

Michaux describes in some detail an individual he met on the Ohio River. This man, who may have been somewhere on the scale between a hunting pioneer and a farming pioneer, was from what is now West Virginia. Traveling alone in a canoe, the frontiersman was on his way to reconnoiter wilderness lands along the Missouri River. "The excellent quality of the land that is reckoned to be more fertile there than that on the borders of the Ohio, and which the Spanish government at that time ordered to be distributed *gratis*, the quantity of beavers, elks, and more especially bisons, were the motives that induced him to emigrate into this remote part of the country," which he would explore before returning to bring out his family. Dressed in a waistcoat and a pair of pantaloons with a large woven sash, the backwoodsman was carrying a carabine, tomahawk, and large knife. "Every evening he encamped on the banks of the river, where, after having made a fire, he passed the night; and whenever he conceived the place favourable for the chace, he remained in the woods for several days together, and with the produce of his sport, he gained the means of subsistence, and new ammunition with the skins of the animals that he had killed."[15]

Michaux continues, "Such were the first inhabitants of Kentucky and Tennessea, of whom there are now remaining but very few." After making their clearings in the forest and defeating the Indians, their "long habit of a wandering and idle life has prevented their enjoying the fruit of their labours, and profiting by the very price to which these lands have risen in so short a time. They have emigrated to more remote parts of the country, and formed new settlements. It will be the same with most of those who inhabit the borders of the Ohio. The same inclination that led them there will induce them to emigrate from it."[16]

Another traveler during this same period, Thaddeus Mason Harris, was a minister from Dorchester, Massachusetts. His *Journal of a Tour into the Territory Northwest of the Allegheny Mountains: Made in the Spring of the Year 1803* contains a description of the hunting pioneers along the Ohio River in what is now West Virginia: "I had often heard a degrading character of the BACK SETTLERS; and had now an opportunity of seeing it exhibited. The abundance of wild game allures them to be huntsmen. They not only find sport in this pursuit, but supply of provisions, together with considerable profit from the peltry. They neglect, of course, the cultivation of the land. They acquire rough and savage manners. Sloth and independence are prominent traits in their character; to indulge the former is their principal enjoyment, and to protect the latter their chief ambition."[17]

Fortescue Cuming, an Englishman who traveled down the Ohio River in 1807, wrote in *Sketches of a Tour to the Western Country, through the States of Ohio and Kentucky,* "It may not be improper to mention, that the backwoodsmen, as the first emigrants from the eastward of the Allegheny mountains are called, are very similar in their habits and manners to the aborigines, only perhaps more prodigal and more careless of life. They depend more on hunting than on agriculture, and of course are exposed to all the varieties of climate in the open air. Their cabins are not better than Indian wigwams."[18]

Cuming quotes one former hunting pioneer as stating

"one man may in one season kill two hundred deer and eighty bears." Cuming later learned that two men had killed one hundred and thirty-five bears in six weeks. That many bear skins, at six to ten dollars each, would have provided a considerable source of money. Unlike the long hunters of an earlier era, these hunters were near enough to traders to make feasible the transporting of these bulky pelts.[19]

When a rainstorm interrupted their journey, Cuming's party stopped along the bank at a dwelling owned by a prosperous farming pioneer family. The travelers received only a sullen reception. However, two hunters who also had stopped there for breakfast spent more than an hour regaling the travelers "with their feats of deer and bear killing, in which the one always related something more extraordinary than the other. At last they bantered each other to go out and kill a deer." Despite the heavy rain, they took up their rifles, put their tomahawks into their belts, and accompanied by a dog headed off into the woods.[20]

Cuming notes that these hunting pioneers often meet to gamble, drink, and fight. Conflicts begin by the most trivial provocations, or sometimes without any at all beyond a desire to test a man's prowess. "Their hands, teeth, knees, head and feet are their weapons, not only boxing with their fists, (at which they are not to be compared for dexterity, to the lower classes in the seaports of either the United States or the British islands in Europe) but also tearing, kicking, scratching, biting, gouging each others eyes out by a dexterous use of a thumb and finger, and doing their utmost to kill each other, even when rolling over one another on the ground; which they are permitted to do by the byestanders, without any interference whatever, until one of the parties gives out, on which they are immediately separated, and if the conqueror seems inclined to follow up his victory without granting quarter, he is generally attacked by a fresh man, and a pitched battle between a single pair often ends in a battle royal, where all present are engaged."[21]

The savagery of backcountry no-holds-barred fighting, and particularly the practice of gouging out an opponent's eye, was commented on by a number of travelers. This type of mayhem was widespread throughout the southern frontier from the Carolinas westward to the Great Plains; it was considerably less prevalent north of the Ohio River. Hunting pioneers, farming pioneers, and particularly riverboatmen were among its most common adherents. The best fighters became local heroes celebrated for their unflinching bravery and toughness in a culture which glorified such traits. As the years went by and more of the gentry arrived on the scene, dueling with pistols became the upper-class counterpart of lower-class, rough-and-tumble fighting, with the same emphasis on unflinching courage in the face of imminent danger.[22]

Cuming was describing hunting pioneers who lived along the Ohio River. The behavior of many of these individuals would have been reinforced by the sometimes wild and unruly lifestyle of the men who worked on the flatboats and keelboats. In general, the boatmen and the hunting pioneers were of the same stock. Although the French had dominated the earlier river trade, records in the post-Revolutionary era show that the overwhelming majority of individuals working on these primitive crafts had English or Scottish (including Scotch-Irish) surnames.[23]

Leaving the Ohio River for a time, Cuming moved south into Kentucky, arriving at Millersburgh, a village of about thirty houses. He and his party stopped for breakfast at Captain John Waller's tavern. Waller had arrived in Kentucky twenty-three years earlier when the area was still a raw frontier and a large portion of the inhabitants would have been hunting pioneers. "He said that buffaloes, bears and deer were so plenty in the country, even long after it began to be generally settled, and ceased to be frequented as a hunting ground by the Indians, that little or no bread was used, but that even the children were fed on game; the facility of gaining which prevented the progress of agriculture, until the poor innocent buffaloes were completely extirpated, and the other wild animals much thinned: And that the principal part of the cultivation of Kentucky had been within the last fifteen years."[24]

Waller told Cuming that at one time the buffalo had been present in herds of several hundred. At the salt licks and springs where the animals congregated, the soil was pressed down to a depth of three or four feet. Buffalo were easy prey for hunters. "Those harmless and unsuspecting animals, used to stand gazing with apparent curiosity at their destroyer, until he was sometimes within twenty yards of them, when he made it a rule to select the leader, which was always an old and fat female. When she was killed, which rarely failed from the great dexterity of the hunter, the rest of the herd would not desert her, until he had shot as many as he thought proper. If one of the common herd was the first victim of the rifle, the rest would immediately fly." Some of the male buffalo exceeded a thousand pounds in weight; females seldom were heavier than five hundred pounds. Waller said this part of Kentucky was originally a canebrake, the bamboo-like growth sometimes extending to a height of forty feet. The cane had been destroyed by the introduction of cattle which ate the tender cane sprouts.[25]

In the meantime, as Kentucky's population had increased rapidly following the Revolutionary War, many of the hunting pioneers and farming pioneers had moved on to other regions. A large portion of them went north of the Ohio River where they joined other frontier families like themselves, some of whom had entered the eastern Ohio country during the Revolutionary War. Those who had arrived earlier, by settling in groups, had survived perilous Indian raiding. As had happened on the frontier during other periods of heightened danger, in the Ohio country from 1775 to 1794 the lifestyles of the hunting pioneers and the farming pioneers tended to become less distinguishable. Anything beyond patch crops was highly vulnerable to destruction by the Indians. As a result, all frontier people in the region had relied heavily on game, supplemented to varying degrees with cattle and hogs which ran loose in the woods. The United States government, while trying to negotiate treaties with the Ohio tribes in the 1780s, had made attempts to remove these frontier people whom they viewed as squatters. Officials wanted to survey the land and offer it for sale to a more "orderly" class of pioneers. Government efforts, both to come to terms with the tribes and to drive off the unwanted hunting pioneers and farming pioneers, were unsuccessful. After peace finally came to the region following the Battle of Fallen Timbers in 1794, the squatters spread westward.[26]

As growing numbers of hunting pioneers and farming pioneers from Kentucky moved into the Ohio country in the late 1790s, they were joined in this northward migration by others from Virginia, the Carolinas, Georgia, Tennessee, and what is now West Virginia. Portions of the southern Ohio wilds were too hilly to be prime agricultural land, but that type of game-filled, wooded terrain was ideal for the needs of the hunting pioneers. Because the soil was sufficient for limited farming, some farming pioneers with modest aspirations also chose these areas.[27]

Increasingly, in the 1790s, a more affluent type of pioneer was coming into the Ohio country, primarily from Pennsylvania, Maryland, Virginia, and New Jersey, with smaller numbers from New York and New England. Most of these new pioneers from the East were farmers who were looking for good agricultural land to purchase and clear, although some were interested in starting commercial and trading centers. Primarily of English, Scotch-Irish, and German stock, they tended to be better educated and to have greater means than the average pioneer, and they were migrating from a much more ordered society. They immediately were distinguishable from the original pioneers by the larger amount of their possessions.[28]

Many of the eastern pioneers followed the hunting pioneers and other squatters down the Ohio River and up its tributaries. They introduced extensive farming, internal improvements, and settlements as they went. Other pioneers coming from the East followed Zane's Trace. This route started at what is now Wheeling, West Virginia, crossed the Ohio River, and traversed the southern Ohio country. At the same time, a considerable number of pioneers from New England began moving directly to an area in northern Ohio immediately south of Lake Erie. Between 1800 and 1810, the non-Indian population of Ohio increased from under fifty thousand to over two hundred thousand.[29]

The hunting pioneers in Ohio had a particular aversion to the farming pioneers who came directly from the East. They considered the earlier farming pioneers to be enough vexation, but the easterners with their altogether different ways seemed far worse. At the root of the problem was their radically different attitude toward wilderness; even more than the other farming pioneers, the easterners seemed avidly anxious to destroy those very same forests which were so essential to the way of life of the hunting pioneers.

In those unusual cases in which the hunting pioneer actually owned the land he lived on, he stood to receive payment from the farming pioneers if he remained long enough. In other instances, the farming pioneer would buy out the hunting pioneer even though the latter did not own the land; in this case the payment was for the "improvements," usually a rough log dwelling and a small amount of cleared land. This compensation might minimize ill feelings, and it also could hasten the departure of these frontiersmen. The most dedicated of the hunting pioneers, however, had moved on without waiting to meet the new arrivals.

John Stillman Wright, a farmer from New York, wrote *Letters From the West; or A Caution to Emigrants*, a book recounting his experiences on the frontier in 1818 and 1819. That portion of his narrative concerning the Cincinnati area is of particular interest, because it illustrates what happened when hunting pioneers lingered too long in an area and were overtaken by the early stages of civilization. The families he describes appear to be starting the transition to a life involving more farming, but they still retain many of the habits of their former lifestyle. They soon would have to join the more restless hunting pioneers who already had departed, or they would become part of a farming society. "The inhabitants however are, mostly, of indolent slovenly habits, devoting the chief part of their time to hunting, and drinking whiskey, (the only liquor in use,) and appear to be a meagre, sickly, spiritless and unenterprising race: contented to live in log-cabins, containing only one room, with the chimney on the outside, and five or six lusty dogs within. Very rarely is a school house or church to be seen, and scarcely a bridge of thirty feet in length. . . . The people, in fact, appear too indolent to raise much grain: they do not usually clear more than thirty or forty acres to a farm; leaving the rest in a state of nature, for the benefit of 'mast and range,' as they express it. . . . Their hogs run at large in the woods, where they keep in tolerably thriving order, and from thence they are taken and killed, as occasion requires, without further feeding."[30]

The great forested wilderness which covered what is now the state of Indiana had a non-Indian population of not much more than two thousand in 1800. Most of these individuals were concentrated in the Vincennes area on the lower Wabash River and to the southeast along the Ohio River and lower Whitewater River. Similar to southern Ohio, portions of southern Indiana consisted of terrain which did not make prime agricultural land. Nevertheless, it was ideal for the hunting pioneers and for some farming pioneers who practiced small-scale agriculture. The rough topography seemed favorable to these frontier people, because it was well drained, contained a large number of springs, and had small valleys which provided enough acreage for their limited crops. The woods supplied both wild game and forage for the stock.[31]

Elias Pym Fordham, whose description of wilderness was quoted near the beginning of this book, wrote in 1817, "Indiana is a vast forest, larger than England, just penetrated in places, by the back-woods settlers, who are half hunters, half farmers." Further on in his account, he expresses a typically Romantic viewpoint: "The forests of Indiana, the mountains of Kentucky, the wilds of Illinois, if they are not so beautiful [as England], yet their grandeur calls forth deeper, more sublime emotions." Everything in these woods "excites the most profound sentiments of adoration for the divine author of Nature,—all call to man the uncertain duration of his existence; but these thoughts are unmixed with aught that can debase his worth or circumscribe his powers. These wildernesses are given to him alone: in them he is free; owning no master but his God, and no authority but that of reason and truth."[32]

William Faux was an English farmer whose book, *Memorable Days in America: Being a Journal of a Tour to the*

United States, relates his travels from 1818 to 1820. After crossing the White River in the southwestern part of Indiana, he "stopped at a quarter-section farmer's who has never cleared nor inclosed any of his land, because sick or idle; being, however, well enough to hunt daily, a sport which, as he can live by it, he likes better than farming, 'and besides,' says he 'we had at first so many wild beasts about us, that we could not keep pigs, poultry, sheep, nor any thing else.'"[33]

An interesting example of a person who appears to have been a hunting pioneer before making the transition to farming pioneer was recorded in *Men and Measures of a Half Century* by Indiana lawyer and banker Hugh McCulloch. In 1833, McCulloch traveled north of Indianapolis through a thick forest where trees nearly a hundred feet tall lined the route. Stopping at a cabin, he was given a meal of fried pork, cornbread, and a strange-tasting beverage which was called tea. After supper he entered into a conversation with his host outside the cabin. McCulloch learned that the frontiersman was a native of North Carolina, from whence he and his wife had migrated to western Pennsylvania. "He remained in Pennsylvania five or six years, until the people became too thick for game, when he moved to Ohio, spent some years in the eastern part of the state, as many more in the western, and thence he had come to Indiana. 'I have been' said he, 'a kinder rolling stone, but I am a good deal better off than when I started. I own eighty acres of good land, twenty acres cleared; a yoke of oxen, a mule, a cart and some farming tools, and besides as good a rifle as you ever laid eyes on.'" The pioneer said he and his wife had eight children and might have two or three more. "'I sha'n't stay here long if I can find anybody to buy me out. Your see, stranger, I am what they call a pierneer, and pierneers oughtn't stay too long in the same place.'"[34]

THE ILLINOIS COUNTRY

The area comprising the present-day state of Illinois is deserving of special attention for its role in the history of the hunting pioneers for three reasons. First, there are more descriptions of these backwoods people in the Illinois wilds than in any other region of the woodland frontier. Second, early Illinois history provides a particularly interesting example of a three-way conflict among the Indians, the hunting pioneers, and the farming pioneers. Third, Illinois is one of the places where the hunting pioneers had an optimum opportunity to fully develop, perfect, and practice their lifestyle over a considerable length of time.

Illinois today does not conjure up visions of wilderness, but that was not the situation prior to the advent of the farming pioneers with their axes and plows. When the hunting pioneers first arrived, the southern and western portions of the Illinois country had a significant tree cover, which was heaviest in broad bands along the watercourses. This forested land, interspersed with prairies of various sizes, was an excellent habitat for wild game. To the north and east there were much greater expanses of prairie, a wilderness of a different kind. The hunting pioneers did not like these wide open areas and intentionally avoided them.

The Illinois country originally had been the domain of the large Illinois tribe. In the 1600s and 1700s, they suffered catastrophic attacks by other tribes, including the Iroquois, Chippewa, Menominee, Winnebago, Sioux, Kickapoo, Potawatomi, Sac, and Fox. By the last decades of the 1700s, these repeated onslaughts had reduced the Illinois tribe to a pitiful remnant, clustered for protection around the old French settlements on the Mississippi River. During this time, some of the aggressor tribes migrated south from what is now Wisconsin and Michigan to take over the area once roamed by the Illinois. The Kickapoo moved to the center of what is now the state of Illinois. The Potawatomi settled near southern Lake Michigan, as well as further south along the Kankakee and Illinois rivers. The Sac and Fox, two closely cooperating tribes, relocated to the extreme northwestern corner of present-day Illinois.[1]

The first American frontiersmen to locate in the Illinois country in any numbers had arrived along the Mississippi River near St. Louis with George Rogers Clark during the Revolutionary War. That conflict saw relatively little fighting between the Indians and the Americans in the Illinois region, due in large part to Clark's diplomatic skills in dealing with the tribes in the area. This was in marked contrast to the extensive warfare which took place between the American frontiersmen and the Indians in other areas west of the Appalachian Mountains during the war, particularly in the Kentucky, Tennessee, and Ohio regions.

Following the Revolutionary War, small numbers of both hunting pioneers and farming pioneers from south of the Ohio River migrated to the southern Illinois country. Most of them joined the frontiersmen already living in the area across the Mississippi River from St. Louis. This low-lying region, which included the old French settlements of Cahokia and

Kaskaskia, came to be known as the American Bottom. The Indians in what is now Ohio and Indiana were impressed by the strength and determination of the United States Army shown at the Battle of Fallen Timbers in 1794. However, the effect of that decisive American victory was not felt to the same extent among the Indians in the Illinois country, where there was little American military presence. At the same time, the tribes in the Illinois country had come to view the pioneers with growing dismay. Sporadic and random attacks on frontier people were made by Kickapoo and Potawatomi warriors, often while these Indians were enroute to or from raids against the Osage Indians across the Mississippi River in the Missouri country.[2]

During the first decade of the 1800s, as the number of people in Kentucky, Tennessee, and Ohio rapidly increased, the population of the Illinois country continued to lag far behind. Its non-Indian residents totaled not much over ten thousand in 1810; many of these inhabitants were of the original French stock. Despite its sparse population, the separate Illinois Territory was created in 1809.

Toward the end of the first decade of the 1800s, under the growing influence of the Shawnee brothers, Tecumseh and the Prophet, most of the Indians throughout the region north of the Ohio River again were growing restless and hostile. More than ever, they viewed the continuous advance of pioneers as a threat to their very existence. The ongoing efforts of the United States government to negotiate treaties in order to obtain the Indians' land added to their concerns. Also, during this time relations between the United States and England were deteriorating rapidly, a situation which would lead to the outbreak of war between those two nations in 1812.

When the War of 1812 started, a majority of the Indians quickly supported the British operating out of Canada, hoping thereby to help turn back the Americans. The warriors assisted the British in the capture of American forts at Michilimackinac in the straits between Lake Huron and Lake Michigan and at Detroit between Lake Erie and Lake Huron. On the shore of Lake Michigan at the isolated outpost of Chicago, warriors defeated and captured the Fort Dearborn command during the garrison's attempted withdrawal eastward. In the Indiana Territory, however, the Indians were unsuccessful in their efforts to capture Fort Wayne and Fort Harrison. As in the Revolutionary War, most of the large-scale fighting on the Trans-Appalachian frontier during the War of 1812 was done elsewhere than in Illinois. In this conflict, the regions of Indiana, Michigan, Ohio, Alabama, and Louisiana saw most of the action, and a large number of the American forces who served in those areas were furnished by Kentucky and Tennessee.

For the hunting pioneers and farming pioneers in the Illinois Territory, the War of 1812 served primarily to increase the incidents of Indian hostility. In most cases, these frontier people were forced to abandon outlying areas and fort-up. Because Illinois was on the periphery of the major fighting, most military operations there were carried out by units recruited locally, with only limited assistance from the federal government or the United States Army. A string of forts was built in the southern Illinois country from which mounted patrols were conducted actively. In addition, a retaliatory campaign into the central portion of the Illinois Territory destroyed Kickapoo and Potawatomi villages and dispersed those Indians. Still, these measures failed to end Indian raiding. Toward the close of the war, American military forces operating out of St. Louis became embroiled in bitter fighting with the Sac and Fox along the Mississippi River near the common border of present-day Illinois and Wisconsin.[3]

After peace between the United States and England was restored in 1815, warfare between the Americans and the Indians ceased. Realizing that their attempts to stop the advance of settlement had failed, the tribes in Illinois returned to their former villages and tried to resume their way of life. Their efforts in the years ahead would meet with only limited success. A key problem would be the pioneers' ongoing depletion of the wild game which had provided the Indians with food, shelter, and clothing. The great buffalo herds of a generation or two earlier were just a memory. Now deer, bear, elk, and other wild game were being killed in increasing numbers by the frontiersmen. This decrease in the number of animals also would mean that the Indians would have difficulty obtaining hides and furs to barter for the trade goods on which they had become dependent. Although the tribes in this region continued to practice their traditional agriculture, they were unwilling to take up the type of full-time farming typical of most pioneers. As a result, they would be forced to rely more and more on government annuities.[4]

For newcomers, who had not known the earlier proliferation of wild game, the numbers of animals in Illinois still seemed impressive. Gershom Flagg, a native of Vermont, migrated westward and established a farm in the southwestern portion of the Illinois country in 1816. In a letter to his brother in December 1817, he writes, "We have a great plenty Deer, Turkies, Wolves, Opossoms, Prairie hens, Eagles, Turky Buzzards, Swans, Geese, ducks, Brant, sand hill Cranes, Parokites & with many other small Animals & birds. . . . There is more honey here in this Territory I suppose than in any other place in the world, I have heard the Hunters say that they have found 8 or 10 swarms a day on the St. Gama & Illinois Rivers where there are no settlements (Truly this must be the Land of Milk & honey.)"[5]

Flagg states that the livestock of the country consists primarily of horses, cattle, and hogs. "There are places in this Territory where Cattle & horses will live all winter & be in good order without feeding, that is upon the Rivers." The hogs grow as fat on hickory nuts, pecans, walnuts, and acorns as any he had seen which were fed on corn. The hogs would have been as numerous as the deer, if it were not for the wolves killing many of the young pigs. The wolves also present a threat to any sheep which might be brought into the region.[6]

Flagg notes that the trees include oak, walnut, basswood, cherry, ash, elm, sassafras, sumac, elder, honey locust, mulberry, crabapple, redbud, pecan, maple, cottonwood, and pawpaw. He explains that the growth of the trees is hampered by frequent fires. "When the fire gets into high thick grass it goes faster than a horse can Run & burns the Prairie smooth."[7]

This was the best of times to be a hunting pioneer in the Illinois wilderness. They could roam the woods and nearby prairies at will with few concerns about encountering Indians intent on taking their lives. Although the hunting pioneers were only one step ahead of the farming pioneers, such as Gershom Flagg, plenty of wilds remained.

Flagg represented a new type of settler in the Illinois country, an easterner. The limited number of farming pioneers from the East who migrated into southern Illinois prior to the 1820s traveled by boat down the Ohio River and settled in among the hunting pioneers and other farming pioneers. As in Ohio and Indiana, the frontier people who had moved into Illinois from Kentucky and other areas were wary of these "Yankees," as easterners were generically called. This feeling in most cases was reciprocated. There usually was little mingling between the hunting pioneers and any eastern farming pioneers, before the former would move on into new wilderness. Even the earlier farming pioneers felt uneasy around the new arrivals. The southern Illinois woods interspersed with prairies were an ideal environment for the hunting pioneers. They made their rough dwellings in the heavy band of trees often miles wide along the watercourses. Situated among oaks, maples, hickories, cottonwoods, and other trees, they had firewood, the shelter of the forest, and access to the wild game which still remained, including deer and bear. The forest floor provided an excellent fruit and nut mast for their hogs, which ran wild. The nearby prairies provided good grazing for their horses and cows. These grassy areas also presented exceptional hunting opportunities. Deer, an increasingly important source of food for both Indians and pioneers after the disappearance of the buffalo, were attracted to the forest margins. There the hunters had both good cover and an optimum view of their prey. The early frontier people in this region, hunting pioneers and farming pioneers alike, generally held the mistaken belief that the soil of the prairies was less fertile than the soil of the deep woods. In addition, the roots of the thick prairie grass were difficult to break through without a heavy plow. Consequently, both types of pioneers usually made clearings in the woods for whatever crops they intended to grow.

In *Sketches of America: A Narrative of a Journey of Five Thousand Miles Through the Eastern and Western States of America*, published in 1818, Englishman Henry Bradshaw Fearon comments, "The inhabitants of Illinois may, perhaps, be ranked as follows: First the Indian hunters, who are neither different in character or pursuits from their ancestors in the days of Columbus. 2d, The 'squatters,' who are half-civilized and half-savage. These are, in character and habits, extremely wretched; indeed, I prefer the genuine uncontaminated Indian." Fearon explains that the third set is composed of farmers, landjobbers, doctors, and lawyers. The fourth group is comprised of some of the old French settlers who possess considerable property.[8]

John Stillman Wright, whose description of the pioneers in the Cincinnati area was quoted in the previous chapter, had continued west into southeastern Illinois. There, in 1818, he beheld an expansive and almost boundless wilderness. The soil rivaled in fertility the land of his native New York. Wright would have settled in this new country but for one factor: the inhabitants (who appear from his description to have been largely hunting pioneers). "They are a motley assemblage of Pennsylvanians, Virginians, Carolinians and Kentuckyans with a few Yankees intermixed, scattered over the face of the country, at the distance of from two to eight or ten miles apart, in order as they say, to have sufficient range for their cattle, and mast for their hogs. At this distance they wish to keep; and they look with a malicious, scowling eye, on the New-England men who settle among them, and begin a course of improvement, by clearing their lands."[9]

At about the same time that Wright was making his observations, this wilderness region of southeastern Illinois, and specifically that area which is now Edwards County, was attracting a very unique group of immigrants. In 1817, Morris Birkbeck and George Flower, two wealthy Englishmen, arrived in the Illinois country with plans to establish a settlement for immigrants from England. They were attracted to this area of woods and prairies not far from the Wabash River, because it reminded them of the park-like estates of the English gentry. Their settlement, known as English Prairie, soon became a magnet for English settlers and travelers. Fortunately for this study of the hunting pioneers, many of these English, including Birkbeck and Flower, wrote books, journals, and letters describing the land and the people who lived there. Nowhere else on the frontier do we have this wealth of detail regarding the hunting pioneers and their lifestyle in the wilderness. Many of the Englishmen took the time and opportunity to observe these backwoods people closely and get past superficial impressions. This process occurred as these settlers and travelers frequently encountered the hunting pioneers in the woods, accompanied them on prolonged excursions in the wilds, and took shelter for the night with them in their rough-hewn cabins.

Birkbeck's *Notes on a Journey from the Coast of Virginia to the Territory of Illinois* gives a description of hunting pioneers leading what he terms a "half-Indian" existence in this land of forests and prairies: "Their habits of life do not accord with those of a thickly settled neighbourhood. They are hunters by profession, and they would have the whole range of the forest for themselves and their cattle.—Thus strangers appear among them as invaders of their privileges; as they have intruded on the better founded exclusive privileges of their Indian predecessors."[10]

Continuing his assessment of these backwoods people, Birkbeck notes, "But there are agreeable exceptions to the coarse part of this general character. I have met with pleasant intelligent people who were a perfect contrast to their semi-Indian neighbours; cleanly, industrious, and orderly: whilst ignorance, indolence, and disorder, with a total disregard of cleanliness in their houses and persons are too characteristic of the hunter tribe."[11]

With a hunting pioneer as a guide, Birkbeck and Flower made an exploratory trip through the area looking for suitable land to purchase. Birkbeck observes that the hunting pioneer families are friendly and share their simple fare with travelers, even though they have to take their corn thirty miles to the nearest mill. Despite having few possessions, they seem comfortable. "To struggle with privations has now become the habit of their lives, most of them having made several successive plunges into the wilderness: and they begin already to talk of selling their 'improvements,' and getting still farther 'back,' on finding that emigrants of another description are thickening about them."[12]

Crossing the Little Wabash River, Birkbeck and his party left all civilization behind. Signs of bear were everywhere. Wandering through the trackless wilderness "where even the sagacity of our hunter-guide had nearly failed us," they finally arrived at the cabin of another hunting pioneer. This dwelling was the third one the frontiersman had built in the past year, "and a very slender motive would place him in a fourth before the ensuing winter. In his general habits, the hunter ranges as freely as the beasts he pursues: labouring under no restraint, his activity is only bounded by his own physical powers; still he is incarcerated—'shut from the common air.' Buried in the depth of a boundless forest, the breeze of health never reaches these poor wanderers; the bright prospect of distant hills fading away into the semblance of clouds, never cheered their sight. They are tall and pale, like vegetables that grow in a vault, pining for light."[13]

Birkbeck and his companions stayed overnight in the hunting pioneer's cabin. This dwelling, which sheltered a very large family, was built of round logs with cracks of three or four inches between them. The roof proved more effective than the roof in most structures of this type, as it protected them fairly well from a drenching rain. Two bedsteads of unhewn logs, with two chairs and a low stool, comprised the entire furnishings. Three rifles, one effective and two which had seen better days, stood in the corners. A fiddle, rarely silent, hung on the wall.[14]

The hunter guide and hunter host became so deeply

engrossed in relating their exploits of the chase that they forgot about eating supper. Although Birkbeck and his party eyed hungrily a great quantity of venison hanging in the smoky fireplace and from the rafters overhead, they hesitated to ask their preoccupied host or less-than-friendly hostess for supper. Instead they contented themselves with some cornbread which they had brought along. After listening to stories of hunting adventures to a late hour, the travelers rolled up in their blankets and went to sleep on a bearskin on the dirt floor of the cabin. In the morning, the hunting pioneers resumed their accounts of the chase until interrupted by the necessary departure of Birkbeck and his party. Before they left, their host finally invited them to partake of some of the venison, and they "all fared sumptuously."[15]

Further on, Birkbeck writes, "These hunters are as persevering as savages, and as indolent. They cultivate indolence as a privilege; 'You English are very industrious, but we have freedom.'" Birkbeck adds that these hunting pioneer families show a "yawning indifference" to nuisances and petty wants which could have been remedied by working "a tenth of the time loitered away in their innumerable idle days." He states that in this life of idleness the Indian is highest on the scale followed by these backwoodsmen.[16]

While Flower stayed on in the area, Birkbeck headed south toward the land office at Shawneetown on the Wabash River to make some entries on land which they had decided to purchase. He traveled "through the wildest of wildernesses" where he encountered a "grave old hunter, who had the air of much sagacity." Birkbeck calls this area, which was flat and swampy, "a dreadful country." He notes that it is "the very solitude" of this land which attracts some backwoods families and causes them to set up temporary habitations.[17]

Apparently, there were exceptions to the desire for

solitude. "At one of these lone dwellings we found a neat, respectable-looking female, spinning under the little piazza at one side of the cabin, which shaded her from the sun." Her husband would be away "on business" for some weeks, and she was "overcome with 'lone.'" During other times of the year, her husband spent much time bear hunting, "which he pursued alone, taking only his dog with him, though it is common for hunters to go in parties to attack this dangerous animal." Last winter he had killed five bears in one week. "The cabin of this hunter was neatly arranged, and the garden well stocked."[18]

Birkbeck observes that wolves and bears are "extremely numerous" and kill many of the hogs which run wild in the swamps. "Bears are lean in summer and very swift of foot, so that dogs can hardly overtake them; but in winter they grow excessively fat on hickory and other kinds of mast, and are unable to run for want of breath; and this is the season of bear-hunting." Bear meat is highly favored, and the skin brings three to five dollars. Neither wolves nor bears attack humans, unless the animal is wounded; then it comes at the hunter in a fury.[19]

Birkbeck calls the hunting pioneers the "true backwoodsmen." He states that he has spent much time with them, staying in their cabins, partaking of their food, and utilizing them as "pilots to explore situations still more remote and which only hunters visit." In his opinion, it is "an ill-chosen or unfortunate attachment to the hunter's life," rather than an aversion to society's regulations, which keeps them aloof from civilization.[20]

"They must live where there is plenty of 'bear and wild honey.' Bear hunting is their supreme delight: to enjoy this they are content to live in all manner of wretchedness and poverty: yet they are not savage in disposition, but honest and kind; ready to forward our wishes and even to labor for us, though our coming will compel them to remove to the 'outside' again."[21]

George Flower wrote of his own wilderness experiences in *History of the English Settlement in Edwards County Illinois, Founded in 1817 and 1818, by Morris Birkbeck and George Flower*: "Early as we were in the occupancy of these prairies, after the Indians had left, there was a class in before us. Not numerous, but of characteristics so peculiar as to deserve a passing notice. They belong to neither savage nor civilized life, but keep their station between the two; following up the Indians as they retreat, and moving away from the farmers as they advance. There were about six of these families scattered over a distance of fifty miles." Flower is writing, of course, of the hunting pioneers.[22]

During Flower's and Birkbeck's exploratory trip referred to earlier, the party's horses turned up missing one morning. While looking for them, Flower became temporarily separated from his companions. He decided to go in search of the dwelling of a Captain Birk (not Birkbeck), whom he earlier heard mentioned as "the oldest settler in these parts; he had been here almost a year."[23]

Flower found Birk outside his cabin, which was adjacent to a small field of corn. The hunting pioneer was not pleased to learn that Flower intended to purchase land in the area. "These original backwoodsmen look upon all new-comers as obtruders on their especial manorial rights. The old hunter's rule is: when you hear the sound of a neighbor's gun, it is time to move away." Flower was impressed with Birk. "I afterward found all of this class of men, who live in solitude and commune so much with nature, relying on their own efforts to support themselves and their families, to be calm, deliberate, and self-possessed whenever they are sober. The best breeding in society could not impart to them more self-possession or give them greater ease of manner or more dignified and courteous bearing."[24]

Flower writes that Birk's cabin is "fourteen feet long, twelve broad and seven high, with earth for a floor" and contains only rough and minimal furnishings. "An ax lay at the door, a rifle stood against the wall. Himself and boys were dressed in buckskin, his wife and three daughters in flimsy calico from the store, sufficiently soiled and not without rents. Mrs. Birk, a dame of some thirty years, was square-built and squat, sallow, and smoke-dried, with bare legs and feet. Her pride was in her hair, which, in two long and well-braided black and shining tails, hung far down her back."[25]

Referring to Captain Birk's participation in the War of 1812, Flower continues, "Birk got his title as commander of a company of men like himself, employed as outlying scouts to the American army on the Canadian frontier." Mrs. Birk seemed less friendly than her husband. Flower attributed this partly to the fact that the British and their Indian allies had been fighting against Captain Birk and the Americans during the recently concluded conflict. Flower knew from past experience that her reaction to English visitors was not unique. "Besides, we came with the intention of settling and bringing other settlers. All this was distasteful to them. They came to enjoy the solitude of the forest and the prairie. . . . Our success would be their defeat and the growth of our colony the signal for their removal." By paying liberally for information and guiding services, and bestowing an occasional dram of whiskey, the English modified these hostile feelings, "and we soon were on friendly terms."[26]

Flower decided to spend the night at the Birks' cabin. "Two or three slices from a half-smoked haunch, a few grams of coarse corn-bread, seasoned by hunger, the best of sauces, gave us a relishing supper." Trying to sleep on the floor,

Flower soon made acquaintance with a large number of fleas. Taking a hogskin, which he refers to as his "not over-luxurious couch," Flower went outside to take his repose on the ground. The next morning the missing horses were found, and he rejoined his companions.[27]

Flower made it clear that he admired many of the hunting pioneers' qualities, but he still noted their less desirable traits. He was particularly grateful for their work in building log cabins for the English to live in temporarily and for supplying them with venison. "In a year or two, they moved into less-peopled regions, or to where there were no people at all, and were entirely lost to this part of the country. The people in this part of Illinois are mostly from the slave-states, from the class of 'poor whites,' so-called." When the hunters traveled to the little towns "on some real or pretended business," they soon got to drinking, "their bane and their ruin." Under the influence, they often became dangerous men. "They own a horse, rifle, ax, and hoe. It is astonishing to see with what dexterity they use a good ax, and how well they shoot with even a bad rifle." He says that despite a lack of industrious habits, they are capable on occasion of working vigorously.[28]

Flower again makes note of the unique demeanor of the hunting pioneers: "Solitude, watchfulness, and contemplation amidst the scenes of nature, from day to day, from week to week, and often from month to month, give them a calm and dignified behavior not to be found in the denizens of civilized life." Some of them do stop moving onward. They increase their corn patch to a field, replace their crude dwelling with a log house, plant a few fruit trees, make other improvements, and "soon arrive at the summit of their desires." He concludes that the only difference between those people who continue the hunting way of life and those who settle down appears to be the intemperance of the former and the sobriety of the latter.[29]

Regarding the individuals who remain addicted to the wilderness hunting life, Flower points out that their days are numbered in that immediate area. English and American settlers interested in owning land were arriving, cutting down trees, and starting more extensive agriculture. "In 1819, the hunter-class of backwoodsmen began to move off, to keep their true position between the receding Indian and the advancing white men. With all their faults, they were an interesting class."[30]

Elias Pym Fordham, whose observations were quoted in earlier chapters, settled briefly at English Prairie. He lists the wild foods as grapes, walnuts, hickory nuts, pecans, pawpaws, raspberries, and strawberries. The game includes bear, deer, raccoon, and beaver, all of which are utilized by the hunting pioneers for food and pelts. There also are turkeys, pheasants, partridges, and prairie hens. In addition, wolves and panthers roam the woods.[31]

Fordham divided the people on this Illinois frontier into different classes. "1st. The hunters, a daring, hardy, race of men, who live in miserable cabins, which they fortify in times of war with the Indians, whom they hate but much resemble in dress and manners. They are unpolished, but hospitable, kind to strangers, honest and trustworthy. They raise a little Indian corn, pumpkins, hogs, and sometimes have a cow or two, and two or three horses belonging to each family: But their rifle is their principal means of support. They are the best marksmen in the world, and such is their dexterity that they will shoot an apple off the head of a companion. Some few use the bow and arrow." After spending much time with these backwoodsmen, Fordham believed "they would sooner give me the shirt off their backs, than rob me of a charge of powder." He states that their conflicts with the Indians have made these frontier people vindictive. "This class cannot be called first Settlers for they move every year or two."[32]

Fordham calls the second class the real settlers. They have more possessions than the first group, but still they "are a half barbarous race." The third class contains doctors, lawyers, storekeepers, farmers, and mechanics. The fourth and highest class consists of rich farmers and wealthy merchants.[33]

After listing and describing the four groups, Fordham singles out the hunting pioneers for his praise. "The prominent feature of their character is power. The young value themselves on their courage, the old on their shrewdness. The veriest villains have something grand about them. They expect no mercy and they shew no fear; 'every man's hand is against them, and their hand is against every man's.'" He explains that these backwoods people show more politeness and genuine kindness than any other people in America. They are polite "for the same reason that the most powerful animals are gentle." He has stayed in their cabins, where venison was roasted on a sharpened stick in the fireplace, and a broken fiddle provided music until past midnight. Having "no regular engagements, night and day are alike to them."[34]

Fordham adds that the hunting pioneer wears buckskin and homespun clothing, a wide belt, and moccasins. He carries a long-bladed knife, tomahawk, powder horn, bullet pouch, and a loaf of Indian corn. He roams the trackless woods depending for his bearings on a kind of instinct rather than a compass. "He is fearless of every thing, attacks every thing that comes in his way, and thinks himself the happiest and noblest being in the world."[35]

Generally viewing most of the hunting pioneers favorably, Fordham also notes certain exceptions: "The hunters on the Missouri are, I am told, a more abandoned set than those on the Wabash. They live entirely under the shelter of a blanket or the bark of trees, and are never nearer to each other than 9 or 10 miles, and moving every week or two. They trap a great many beavers and by this are enabled to buy spirits. They are more like the amphibious race on the banks of the Ohio, who are by turns hunters, boatmen, and farmers, and to whom robbing, violence and even murder are familiar."[36]

William Faux, who was quoted in reference to the hunting pioneers in Indiana, writes of their counterparts at English Prairie: "Armstrong, a hunting farmer, this day shot four deer, while he is too idle to inclose his corn-field, which is devoured by cattle and horses, save when a boy watches it to keep them off. This man and family then, though with plenty of land, must buy corn, and depend upon wild meat for the support of his idle family, who have either a feast or famine."[37]

Faux also relates what may or may not have been an isolated or extreme example of the hunting pioneers' behavior toward the English. "The hunters, or Illinois Rowdies, as they are called, are rather troublesome. . . . One of a large offended party came drunk to Mr. Flower's house, and said, he would enter and shoot him. Mr. Flower got his rifle and pointed it at the fellow, on which he rushed up and put his mouth madly to the muzzle, and said, 'Fire.'" Flower then put his rifle down, and the hunter was dragged away by some members of the group who were less inebriated. Near the end of his journal, Faux makes this additional observation on frontier life: "I am now living on wild bucks and bears, mixed up, and barbarizing with men almost as wild as they: men, systematically unprincipled, and in whom the moral sense seems to have no existence: this is the lot of all coming here."[38]

William Newnham Blane, who is described as "an English gentleman" on the title page of *An Excursion Through the United States and Canada During the Years 1822-23*, provides detailed descriptions of the hunting pioneers in the

English Prairie area. He states that the worst vices of the backwoodsmen are "drinking, fighting, etc., and, when fighting, 'gouging' and biting." He says fighting in the backwoods "is only worthy of the most ferocious savages. The object of each combatant is to take his adversary by surprise; and then, as soon as he has thrown him down, either to 'gouge' him, that is, to poke his eye out, or else to get his nose or ear into his mouth and bite it off. . . . This abominable practice of gouging is the greatest defect in the character of the Backwoodsmen."[39]

Traveling during the winter near the English Prairie area, Blane came to a dangerous ford on the Fox River. He was preparing to enter the freezing water, when three hunting pioneers appeared "in hunting shirts, and had with them their rifles, tomahawks, and knives." They assisted him in crossing the river at another place on some driftwood, and his horse was driven across at the ford. As night was fast approaching, one of the hunters offered to let the Englishman stay at his cabin. Proceeding through woods and prairies, Blane considered how easy it would be for these men to murder him and take his horse, saddlebags, watch, and money; he was a perfect stranger, and no one would have inquired about him. He later learned from experience in the wilderness that such concerns were "entirely groundless," because he never encountered any danger from these backwoods people.[40]

Blane found the hunting pioneer's dwelling to be "a miserable log cabin of only one room," and there was no shelter of any kind for his horse. The cabin was made of large, rough logs notched at the ends. A big stone fireplace took up most of one wall. "When, of an winter's evening, the back of the fire-place is filled with a great log called the 'back log,' and is piled up with large billets of wood, it forms a very comfortable and cheering spectacle." These cabins usually

were built in a small clearing in the forest. Blane makes note of
the common practice of girdling the nearby trees with an ax
and then burning the trunks. This kills the trees and causes
them to resemble large charcoal pillars.[41]

"The first who penetrate the woods, and who dwell on
the very frontiers of civilization, are the Hunters. These men
lead a wandering life, much resembling that of their occasional
companions, the Indians. They subsist almost entirely on game;
and what little money they make is obtained by the sale of furs,
etc. As soon as the country begins to be settled, and when,
consequently, game becomes scarce, the Hunters break up their
habitations, and move further off."[42]

Blane points out that others often speak ill of these
hunters, but he does not agree with this opinion. He admits that
some disreputable people have fled from justice and taken up a
hunting mode of life; but "they have no right to the title of
Hunters," because they do not have the true hunter's highly
developed skills. "For my own part, and as far as my own
observations go, I shall always speak well of the real Hunters;
for I have invariably found them open-hearted and very
hospitable. Their manner of life, indeed, makes them, in some
degree, partake of the Indian character, though they by no
means have the same nobleness of sentiment, and high sense of
honor."[43]

Blane calls the next class squatters. He says some of
these individuals earlier had been hunters, "who, from the
increase of their families, can no longer pursue their former
mode of life." He says all squatters, whether originally hunters
or not, are fond of hunting and kill a large amount of game, but
they do not depend upon it for their survival as do the true
hunters.[44]

While the immigrants from England were moving into
English Prairie and displacing hunting pioneer families,

hunting pioneers in other regions of southern Illinois also were moving on into new wilderness under pressure from other farming settlers. Some of these hunting pioneers arrived in the wilds near present-day Springfield just prior to 1820 and built their cabins in the belts of woods along the rivers and streams. William Vipond Pooley's long article published in 1908, "The Settlement of Illinois From 1830 to 1850," includes a description of the years leading up to 1830: "Here in this Sangamon country the hunter-pioneer found an ideal land and here we find the re-enactment of the scenes of the first settlement in the extreme southern portion of the state."[45]

John Mack Faragher's study of this area in his book, *Sugar Creek: Life on the Illinois Prairie*, certainly supports this view. Faragher follows the life of Robert Pulliam who moved in 1819 with his wife and family from southwestern Illinois to Sugar Creek, a tributary of the Sangamon River. Pulliam, of Scotch-Irish ancestry, was born in the Blue Ridge area of Virginia in 1776 and grew up in Kentucky before migrating to the Illinois country in 1796. Marrying in 1804, he hunted, raised patch crops, herded cattle, and let his hogs run wild in the woods. In 1808, he lost a leg in a hunting accident. Pulliam was attracted to the Sugar Creek area, in part, because the interspersed woods and prairies made it a hunter's paradise. There was wood for shelter and fuel, a thick mast beneath the trees for hogs, good grazing for cattle, and plenty of wild game. Many of the hunting pioneers in this area would move on, but others stayed and eventually entered the ranks of permanent farmers.[46]

This settlement of the Sangamon country in the 1820s occurred at the same time that most of the Kickapoo, under growing pressure from pioneers and the United States government, were in the process of departing from Illinois for the Trans-Mississippi West. However, two bands, each including 250 warriors, refused to leave. One of these groups, living in the Peoria Lake area of central Illinois, raided as far south as the Sangamon country. No longer attacking frontier people, the Indians now limited their marauding to killing cattle and hogs, and stealing horses. Such Kickapoo raiding would continue throughout the decade.[47]

The hunting pioneers continued to move northward into central Illinois. Not far behind them came the southern farming pioneers and rapidly increasing numbers of farmers from the East. Lois A. Carrier, in *Illinois: Crossroads of a Continent*, writes that the most serious complaint of the backwoodsman was the number of Yankees in the state. The dissension between the two groups was rooted in their widely divergent attitudes toward the wilderness. The hunting pioneers were enamored of the wilds and viewed them as a sanctuary. The Yankees, on the other hand, were anxious to replace the wilderness with farms and cities.[48]

Despite the increase of easterners in central Illinois, pioneers coming from the south remained in the majority there for some years. Regarding the hunting pioneers in the area of present-day Peoria, seventy miles north of the Sangamon area, Pooley observes, "In character the population was the same as that of the Sangamon country, for the settlements along the Illinois river were only outgrowths of the older Sangamon settlements. The Kentuckians and Tennesseans appeared frequently as in the southern Illinois country taking possession of the timberlands and leading a half-hunter, half-farmer life."[49]

As the hunting pioneers continued to move on, they still were finding extensive woods along the rivers and streams, but they also were encountering a region with greater expanses of prairies. A. D. Jones, a native of New England, wrote his observations of this area in *Illinois and the West*, published in 1838: "It is called a level, flat country, and it is, compared to the eastern states, but not as level as it has been described." He reports that the land presents a continual change of levels with sloughs, high knolls, and deep ravines. "The timber on the 'bottoms' is dense and heavy, and tangled with a most luxuriant growth of vines, shrubs, briars, and rank grass. These bottoms are on all the rivers and creeks, skirting the prairies and making beautiful belts running in every direction through the country." Jones describes the bluffs along the rivers as "but upon one side in a place, while on the opposite lie the heavy timbered bottom lands from a mile to six in width." He says the prairies are of two types: flat or rolling, the latter having swells twenty to sixty feet high between which are low and swampy sloughs. The grass sometimes can reach "the top of a man's head as he sits on his horse."[50]

The hunting pioneers kept pushing further north, following the wooded lands bordering the Illinois and Mississippi rivers and their tributaries, but continuing to avoid the large prairies. Pooley notes, "The pioneer of the Illinois frontier was still of the hunter type. He was primarily a woodsman who had come to the new country with his rifle, axe and hunting knife prepared to attack the problem of the frontier in the same way his ancestors had attacked it in Kentucky and Tennessee generations before. He changed little before 1830, for his cautious contact with the small prairies of the South gave him little real capital with which to attack the broader expanses of the North. Practically shut off from the prairie, he followed the woodlands until the outbreak of the Black Hawk War in 1832, which date marks the beginning of a sudden and sharp transition in pioneer characteristics."[51]

The Black Hawk War was the result of the mounting pressure the hunting pioneers and farming pioneers were placing on the Sac and Fox living in the northwestern corner of Illinois. Eventually, some of the pioneers began agitating and petitioning for the removal of these Indians from the state. August Kennerly, an agent working for Indian Superintendent William Clark, wrote to his superior that it seemed to be the consensus "of the better class of people, that the petition had been got up by some of that portion of the inhabitants who, being too indolent to work, depend chiefly upon hunting for their support, and who resorted to that method to save the game, and get the Indians out of the way, as being too greatly their superiors in hunting the wild game of the forest."[52]

The Sac chief, Black Hawk, initially hoped that those Indians wanting to retain their ancestral lands in Illinois could defy the American pioneers and the United States government peacefully by presenting a united front and by obtaining British support from Canada. Instead, an onrush of events in 1832 brought an outbreak of fighting between the Indians and the Americans which would be known as the Black Hawk War. The Sac and Fox, aided by some Kickapoo and a limited number of Potawatomi and Winnebago (the latter from the southern Wisconsin area), briefly stopped the advance of the frontier people and even forced them to retreat southward. In general, the hunting pioneers and farming pioneers did not distinguish themselves in this initial fighting. Black Hawk, however, was unable to attract enough Potawatomi and Winnebago to sustain his cause, and he received no aid from Canada. As a result, he and his followers were defeated overwhelmingly by a large force of United States soldiers and militia. The surviving Sac and Fox were relocated west of the Mississippi River, and soon they would be followed by the Potawatomi and the last remnants of the Kickapoo.[53]

This final victory over the Indians in northern Illinois had immediate repercussions for the hunting pioneers. With the end of the Black Hawk War, a large migration of farming pioneers from the eastern states got underway before the hunting pioneers could regain their northward momentum. Instead of coming to Illinois via the Ohio River, as had been the case in earlier years, the easterners now were arriving primarily on steamboats via the Great Lakes.[54]

This new wave of settlement by easterners in northern and central Illinois accomplished what the Indians had been unable to do: it permanently ended the northward advance of the hunting pioneers by destroying the wilderness on which the backwoodsmen depended. These easterners had never lived in the wilderness, and they had no desire to do so now. They wanted only to civilize it. The new pioneers took up unoccupied timberland as well as open prairie. The trees were chopped down, and heavy plows effectively cut through the thick roots of the prairie grass. These settlers were full-time farmers; for them hunting furnished only supplemental provisions. Eventually, the pursuit of what little game remained would be viewed by many of the more affluent primarily as sport.

Eliza W. Farnham's book, *Life in Prairie Land*, illuminates the situation on the Illinois frontier at this time. Departing from her native New York in 1836, she traveled extensively in Illinois during the next four years. Farnham describes the original pioneers from "the dense forests of Ohio and Pennsylvania, the undulating hills of Kentucky, and the old homes of Virginia" who had displaced the Indians. These people, she says, were not ready to work "with the steady perseverance which anticipates its reward," when instead nature invited them to "enjoy every passing hour." They were content to live in a rude cabin with a single field; more than that was unnecessary. In their view, added work only burdened the spirit and made slaves of free men. "But a dark shadow soon fell upon his home. Files of earnest men, with hard hands and severe, calculating faces, pressed toward it from the east."[55]

The new eastern settlers moved in around the hunters, and "their axe was heard in the neighboring grove." They built more elaborate cabins, erected barns, and fenced fields. These new additions to the landscape were visible wherever the hunters went. "If he chased the deer or hunted the grouse, or was returning from a visit to a neighboring settlement, there they stood, the first objects that greeted his vision; a blight upon the fair scene whose free aspect he had never thus marred." He did not like the crowded feeling, the busy sounds which came early in the day from his neighbor's home, nor his neighbor's hard work, his large crops, nor anything about that "toilsome life."[56]

The pressure to depart, "following those who fled before him," rapidly escalated as the Yankees offered to pay the hunting pioneer for his cabin and field. Everything combined to tell him that he must leave. "He therefore gathers his few worldly goods, and these, except his horses and rifle, are more than he wishes they were, and turns from his deserted hearthside to seek a more congenial spot, where industry and trade have not yet despoiled the fair earth, or crowded it with busy, thriving homes." Now a permanent population takes over. Broad farms with "stately houses take the place of the solitary cabin; and industry, that counts her gains, has stretched her transforming arm over all the fair land. The wild, the free, the mysterious, are fading beneath her touch."[57]

Concluding our descriptions of the hunting pioneers in the Illinois wilderness as seen by their contemporaries, we come to William Oliver's *Eight Months in Illinois*. Oliver, an Englishman, arrived in Illinois in 1842. His account is of particular interest for the portrait it paints of some of the remaining hunting pioneers just prior to the total demise of their way of life in that state. "The hunter of the West generally follows his occupation on horseback; and a more picturesque turn-out, or one more in keeping with the accompanying scenery, is not often to be met with. He generally wears a broad-brimmed palmetto hat, covering a profusion of hair, which flows over his neck and shoulders. His face, tanned by exposure to all weathers, is often garnished by a beard, untouched by razor or scissors for many weeks, and his throat, unless the weather is severe, is unfettered by a neckcloth." He wears a blanket coat, homemade trousers, and high boots. "Slung over his shoulder is a bullet pouch made of leather, or of the furred skin of some wild animal, ornamented with sundry tags and fringes, accompanied by a powder flask, made of a fine horn, and polished so thin, that the grains of powder can be seen through it; a charge or powder measure, made of horn or bone, with an attempt at carving upon it, and often with the initials of the owner's name; and a tomahawk, with its head enclosed in a leather case. In the front part of the belt which sustains the last-mentioned articles, is a sheath containing a large knife. The other shoulder is occupied by a heavy rifle, with a barrel of fifty inches long, stocked forward to the muzzle, and mounted with brass." The butt is crescent-shaped to fit tightly into the arm near the shoulder and thus support some of the weight of the long barrel. "The horse, like its rider, is 'unkempt, unshorn,' with flowing mane and tail, caparisoned with a double-reined bridle with Spanish bit, heavy and plated with brass, and a Spanish saddle with heavy brass stirrups; a blanket being folded for a saddle cloth." Oliver adds a significant footnote: "This description applies to the best appointed of those hunters who have remained among the settlements. The hunter on the frontier settlements is often clothed in a hunting shirt, leggings, and moccassins of tanned deer skin."[58]

Oliver continues his narrative on the hunting pioneers: "Riding leisurely along the outskirts of the prairie-girt grove, he is seen to stop at a point commanding a view of some sweeping vista enbayed in the dark woods, like the arm of the sea, with many winding channels of green among the bosky islands of hazel, sumac, and sassafrass. Long and patiently he stands searching the openings with his practiced eye to catch a glimpse of the browsing deer." If a deer is sighted, the hunter dismounts and moves closer on foot, taking advantage of undulations in the ground or vegetation to conceal his approach. Usually he is sure of hitting his target if he can get within 120 or 130 paces.[59]

"The Kentucky rifle I have in some measure described above, yet I may add a few particulars, seeing the weapon has acquired some celebrity. Whatever the calibre may be, the barrel is very rarely below forty-five inches, much more frequently forty-eight or fifty, and sometimes longer than that, and often so heavy, that to hold it out steadily, requires an arm of no little strength." Rifles of approximately .50 caliber are used for hunting large animals; guns of smaller calibers are employed in shooting squirrels, turkeys, and other small game.[60]

It is evident that not all of the rifles used by hunting pioneers in this area were made by skilled gunsmiths. Oliver states that some of the barrels burst despite their thickness, "a circumstance which, to me, appeared quite mysterious, until I detached one from the long stock, which completely covers the lower side of the barrel, when the mystery was solved. It would appear that the barrels are made from a bar of iron, the edges of which are brought together, and welded,—a process which might answer well enough if the welding were efficiently performed, which it never had been in any instance that came under my notice; but, on the contrary, was sometimes so badly done, that it was surprising that the gun ever withstood the shock of a single discharge." The locks were frequently cheap, and they often snapped without igniting the charge. Adding to the problem, these hunters used inferior flints found along the banks of creeks, instead of buying good ones.[61]

Oliver observes that the hunting pioneers spend much time experimenting to find the proper gunpowder charge, usually firing into a tree from which the rifle balls are then cut out with an ax. This process is repeated every time the frontiersman obtains a new supply of powder. The rifle ball is wrapped in a greased linen patch; it fits just loosely enough in the barrel so that it can be rammed down easily. In preparing to fire, the rifleman sets his feet wide apart with most of his weight on the right leg; the right elbow then is raised high, and the left arm is extended to its full length along the stock. "At the commencement of taking aim, the muzzle is considerably depressed; but, on the sights being arranged, is gradually raised, with a motion decreasing till it terminates, and the gun is discharged at the same instant."[62]

It is Oliver's overall assessment of the hunting pioneers which is particularly fitting to bring to a close their era in the Illinois country: "The hunter is always poor, and in some measure despised by his more industrious neighbours; and when a man once acquires a habit of wandering in the pathless wilderness in search of game, it takes such hold of him that he very rarely shakes it off; indeed the occupation requires a vigilance so absorbing, as speedily to characterize his whole manner." Oliver notes that the hunter's eye is never at rest, but continuously moves intently from object to object and repeatedly surveys the surroundings. This behavior occurs not only in the forest, but even inside a house.[63]

"The real hunter is the pioneer of American civilization. He is the first to dispute the possession of the wilderness with the red man and with the wild denizens of the forest, and in some measure, like them, is intolerant of the near approach of a population, bringing with it the trammels and interruptions of civilized institutions." Annoyed by the hated sound of an ax in the woods or the smoke of the settler's fire, "he with his family seeks a more congenial home in those solitudes where nature still holds undisputed sway." In following this course, the hunting pioneer is doing only what to him is most agreeable. "He was born in solitude. . . . His associations are not tinctured with the busy crowds and homes of cities, but with the still solitudes of the primeval forest." He does not philosophize on the destinies of the crowded masses, but muses while wandering the banks of some great river which rolls on into regions unknown.[64]

"Your true hunter is often a simple-minded, unaffected child of nature; true he is ignorant, but this ignorance includes the follies and very many of the vices of civilized life. The worst example of his tribe is he who has not fled before the influx of population, and who, impatient of the restraints of industrious habits, has generally reaped nothing from civilization beyond its vices and its scorn."[65]

Thus, in northern Illinois, the hunting pioneers ran out of time and space east of the Mississippi River. The great numbers of easterners were followed by many immigrants coming directly from England, Scotland, Ireland, Germany, Norway, Sweden, and Denmark. In the meantime, the route for the more determined hunting pioneers would lead across the Mississippi River into Missouri, Arkansas, eastern Oklahoma, Louisiana, and eastern Texas, where some forest wilderness still remained.

6

THE SOUTH AND ACROSS THE MISSISSIPPI

The previous two chapters examined the hunting pioneers and their wilderness domain in present-day West Virginia, Kentucky, Ohio, Indiana, and Illinois. In this chapter, the focus turns first to the hunting pioneers in the deep woods of Tennessee, Alabama, and Mississippi. Then, the account will move across the Mississippi River and follow these backwoods families into the forests of Missouri, Arkansas, eastern Oklahoma, Louisiana, and eastern Texas.

In *The Dixie Frontier: A Social History of the Southern Frontier from the First Transmontane Beginnings to the Civil War*, Everett Dick explains that the general characteristics of the hunting pioneers were the same from Illinois to Alabama. However, the warmer weather in the south provided an easier environment. It enabled the hunting pioneers to utilize temporary shelters for longer periods. It also allowed them to construct cabins with less concern for keeping out extreme cold. Evidence of the hunting pioneer's main activity was everywhere: antlers, horns, hides, and fur skins were both outside and inside the cabin. A pack of dogs kept for hunting and to warn of Indians greeted the visitor. As in the north, after the buffalo were killed off, deer and bear became the favored game, along with hogs which had been allowed to run wild in the woods.[1]

The most famous individual associated with the southern wilderness was Davy Crockett. He led a hunting pioneer type of life only briefly, but in the public mind Crockett always will be linked with that lifestyle. Crockett and Daniel Boone were born a half-century apart, but the lives and legends of the two men contain many similarities. In addition to time spent as hunting pioneers, both men engaged in other occupations which were decidedly uncharacteristic of that group. Although Boone and Crockett became more prominent in the social order than the ordinary hunting pioneer, it was the portion of their lives spent primarily in pursuit of wild game which made both men famous. Boone's exploits occurred near the beginning of the era of the hunting pioneers; Crockett's came toward the end. As was the case with Boone, Crockett's life and legend have influenced greatly the general public's conception of life on the Trans-Appalachian wilderness frontier.

It is significant that in the late 1880s when Theodore Roosevelt and other wealthy sportsmen established an organization of "American hunting riflemen," it was named The Boone and Crockett Club. The first three objectives of the club were: "1) To promote manly sport with the rifle; 2) To promote travel and exploration in the wild and unknown, or but partially known, portions of the country; 3) To work for the preservation of the large game of this country, and so far as possible to further legislation for that purpose, and to assist in enforcing the laws." It is easy to envision Boone and Crockett approving of the first two objectives, but their often wanton destruction of wild game would seem at odds with the preservationist sentiments of the third.[2]

Crockett was born in 1786 in what is now eastern Tennessee. After marrying, he spent some years farming in that region. In 1811, he moved with his family to the middle of the state, where he apparently was able to spend more time hunting and less time tending crops. Of this area he later wrote in his autobiography, "I found this a very rich country, and so new that game of different sorts was very plenty. It was here that I began to distinguish myself as a hunter, and to lay the foundation for all my future greatness; but mighty little did I know of what sort it was going to be. Of deer and smaller game I killed abundance; but the bear had been much hunted in those parts before, and were not so plenty as I could have wished."[3]

Crockett served in the militia as a scout during the War of 1812, but he did not take part in any of the major battles on the southern frontier during that conflict. For two decades following the war, he embarked on a varied career which included election to local, state, and national offices. During this period, it was the limited time Crockett spent living and hunting deep in the wilderness which seemed to give him particular pleasure.

In the early 1820s, Crockett migrated into western Tennessee. This was an area of very rugged terrain, partly due to the New Madrid earthquakes of 1811 and 1812. These gigantic convulsions devastated and radically altered much of the landscape, uprooting trees and changing the course of rivers. The whole area was teeming with wild game of all descriptions, especially bears. Crockett and his hunting companions killed 105 bears during a period of seven months.[4]

Crockett and his family lived where the nearest house was seven miles away, and the next nearest was fifteen miles. Of this area he observes, "It was complete wilderness, and full of Indians who were hunting. Game was plenty of almost every kind, which suited me exactly, as I was always fond of hunting." While out with his dogs one day, he saw "about the biggest bear that ever was seen in America. He looked, at the distance he was from me, like a large black bull." Crockett and the dogs pursued the bear into a "roaring thicket," where it climbed a large oak tree. The bear was shot twice; the second shot brought the animal down. Crockett continues, "I took my tomahawk in one hand, and my big butcher-knife in the other, and run up within four or five paces of him at which he let my dog go, and fixed his eyes on me. I got back in all sorts of a hurry, for I knowed if he got hold of me, he would hug me altogether too close for comfort. I went to my gun and hastily loaded her again, and shot him the third time which killed him good."[5]

Crockett's reputation as a prolific hunter made him a legend during his lifetime, a considerable attainment in an era of unrestricted hunting. Much more of a self-promoter than Boone had been, Crockett emphasized this backwoods image in an attempt to further his political career. He was too late on the Trans-Appalachian frontier to match even closely the significance of Boone's role in that region, but Crockett's later death at the Alamo on the Trans-Mississippi frontier would ensure him a lasting place in the pantheon of American heroes.

John James Audubon, the famous ornithologist, naturalist, and painter traveled widely on the frontier; he was in the South during the early 1820s. In *Delineations of American Scenery and Character*, Audubon gives a detailed account of meeting a hunting pioneer and his family in the wilderness of northwestern Mississippi. One of the interesting aspects of this narrative is that the man Audubon describes was a native of New England, a rarity among hunting pioneers. "In the course of one of my rambles, I chanced to meet with a squatter's cabin on the banks of the Cold Water River. In the owner of this hut, like most of those adventurous settlers in the uncultivated tracts of our frontier districts, I found a person well versed in the chase, and acquainted with the habits of some of the larger species of quadrupeds and birds." Audubon entered into a discussion with the man regarding the animals in the vast adjacent swamp. "He told me he thought it the very place I ought to visit, spoke of the game which it contained, and pointed to some bear and deer skins, adding that the individuals to which they had belonged formed but a small portion of the number of those animals which he had shot within it." The hunting pioneer agreed to accompany Audubon through the swamp and invited him to stay the night in his cabin.[6]

Audubon adds, "The quietness of the evening seemed in perfect accordance with the gentle demeanor of the family." The wife and children, intrigued with Audubon's vocation of going about in search of birds and plants, asked him many questions. "The husband, a native of Connecticut, had heard of the existence of men such as myself, both in our own country and abroad, and seemed greatly pleased to have me under his roof. Supper over, I asked my kind host what had induced him to remove to this wild and solitary spot. 'The people are growing too numerous now to thrive in New England,' was his answer. . . . The conversation then changed, and the squatter, his sons and myself, spoke of hunting and fishing, until at length tired, we laid ourselves down on pallets of bear skins, and reposed in peace on the floor of the only apartment of which the hut consisted."[7]

The family recently had been plagued by a cougar (usually called panther or painter by the locals), which was killing their semiwild hogs and cattle in the woods. Audubon offered to help kill the cougar. He was told that any attempt would be futile, unless some neighbors and their dogs joined them. The hunting pioneer soon contacted the neighbors, "several of whom lived at a distance of some miles, and appointed a day of meeting."[8]

At the chosen time, five hunters made their appearance at the cabin; they were accompanied by "large ugly curs" similar to those of Audubon's host. The men were mounted on unimpressive-looking horses, but no horses were better suited for pursuing cougar or bear through rough terrain. Reaching the edge of the swamp, the riders dispersed through the thick woods looking for fresh tracks. The sounding horn of one hunter announced success. The dogs headed for the interior of the swamp where they treed the cougar. One of the men fired and hit the cat, but the shot was not fatal. Leaping to the ground, the quarry took off again with the hunting party following right behind. Finally, the horses were so exhausted that the riders dismounted and continued the chase on foot. For two more hours the hunters and dogs pursued the cougar through the wilds before the animal was treed again. Three rifles were fired in unison, and the panther fell to the ground. Attacked by the dogs, "the infuriated cougar fought with desperate valour" until it was dispatched with a last shot.[9]

Audubon describes what he says are the three modes of hunting deer, calling them "Still Hunting," "Firelight Hunting," and "Driving." "Still hunting is followed as a kind of trade by our frontier men. To be practiced with success, it requires great activity, and expert management of the rifle, and a thorough knowledge of the forest, together with an intimate acquaintance with the habits of the Deer, not only at different seasons of the year, but also at every hour of the day, as the hunter must be aware of the situations which the game prefers, and in which it is most likely to be found, at any particular time." The "Still Hunter," whom Audubon calls the true hunter, wears a hunting shirt, trousers, belt, and moccasins, all made of leather, and carries a rifle, knife, and tomahawk. Setting off, he searches for recent sign. When tracks are found, the pursuer travels rapidly until he begins to close in on the object of his chase; he then moves with caution from tree to tree. Finally sighting the deer, the hunter eases nearer until he can fire and kill the animal. In "Firelight Hunting," pine knots are used for illumination at night. The hunter moves forward; a person immediately behind him holds the torch. They continue on until they see the deer's eyes shining in the darkness. The animal remains motionless in the light, while the men proceed close enough to discern its form. The hunter then fires his weapon and kills his prey. The third method, "Driving," would not have been used very often by hunting pioneers. It involved men pressing the deer forward to a stand where the hunter waited.[10]

As the hunting pioneers spread throughout the woods of the lower south, they sometimes were followed by herders and drovers, people who shared with them not only a love of hunting but a bias against farming. It seems that these herders and drovers were distinguished from the hunting pioneers primarily by a tendency to rely more on cattle and hog raising and to depend somewhat less on the pursuit of wild game. As the years went by, it is likely that some of the hunting pioneers would have adopted the pastoral ways of the drover, while still rejecting the more settled life of the farmer. Those hunting pioneers who were committed wholeheartedly to their way of life, however, would have moved on in search of new wilderness.

Also at this time in the South, the cotton-based plantation system was taking hold. These plantations, as well as smaller farms producing other crops, required the destruction of the wilderness. Under the pressure from this advancing agricultural frontier, the life of the southern hunting pioneer would come to an end east of the Misssissippi River by the 1830s.

Meanwhile, in the 1790s, the dynamic of American westward expansion had been making its influence felt across

the Mississippi River. At that time, most of the non-Indian
inhabitants of the present-day states of Louisiana, Arkansas,
and Missouri were French families engaged in hunting and the
fur trade. Some of them had settled there during the first half of
the 1700s, a time of competition with Spain for control of this
region west of the Mississippi River. These French people
stayed on under Spanish rule after France was forced to give up
her colonial ambitions in North America in 1763 as a result of
the treaty which ended the French and Indian War. Soon after,
when the English took over the former French settlements east
of the Mississippi River, some of those French inhabitants,
preferring Spanish to English rule, also moved westward.

By the last decade of the 1700s, this Spanish domain
was drawing a considerable number of hunting pioneers and
farming pioneers, primarily from Kentucky and Tennessee.
The Spanish had adopted a policy of permitting Americans to
settle in their territory on a controlled basis. They believed that
if they gradually allowed some of the frontiersmen to enter
legally, Spanish lands would not be overrun forcibly by a large
onrush of American pioneers at a later date. Chafing under the
loss of his lands and the "overcrowding" east of the Mississippi
River, Daniel Boone was among the individuals considering
new opportunities to the west during this period. Knowing of
Boone's favorable reputation, the Spanish were eager to have
him settle in their domain.[11]

Upon his arrival with his family in present-day
Missouri in 1799, Boone was appointed as a local official in
the area west of St. Louis, a region which was attracting many
American pioneers. Mindful of what had happened to him in
Kentucky, Boone made efforts to obtain legal title to property
through a Spanish land grant. In 1803, when the United States
acquired the vast area of the Louisiana Purchase, which
included the Missouri country, a question arose over whether

or not Boone had fulfilled the requirements of the grant. Finally, after years of legal complications and controversy, Boone's Spanish land grant was confirmed in 1814 by a special act of the United States Congress.[12]

After moving to Missouri, Boone was a frequent visitor at a nearby Shawnee village, whose inhabitants had migrated from east of the Mississippi River. Boone knew many of them from those earlier days. The Indians, in turn, visited him at his home. Boone also joined the Shawnee on short hunts. His attitude toward the Indians, which was always in contrast to that of the majority of hunting pioneers, was all the more noteworthy in view of the loss of his two sons and the kidnapping of his daughter at their hands.[13]

Although Boone's continuing interest in owning land and holding public office set him apart from the typical hunting pioneers in the Missouri country, he remained one of them at heart and maintained his roaming and hunting ways despite his advancing years. He and his sons, Nathan and Daniel, went on extended hunts in the wilds of the Ozark plateau; it was like the early days of the Kentucky country all over again. For several years after their arrival, the extended Boone family derived most of their income from the sale of hides and furs.[14]

In 1816, when Boone was 82 years of age, an army officer stationed at Fort Osage on the western edge of the Missouri country wrote, "We have been honored by a visit from col. Boone, the first settler of Kentucky; he lately spent two weeks with us. . . . The colonel cannot live without being in the woods. He goes a hunting twice a year to the remotest wilderness he can reach; and hires a man to go with him, whom he binds in written articles to take care of him, and bring him home, dead or alive. He left this for the River Platt, some distance above." Boone died four years later at the age of 86. The old hunter had come to the end of his wilderness days.[15]

Recollections of the Last Ten Years, Passed in Occasional Residences and Journeyings in the Valley of the Mississippi, written by Timothy Flint, a Presbyterian minister from Massachusetts, chronicles his observations in the decade following the War of 1812. During half of that time he lived on the outskirts of St. Louis. Referring to the pioneers whom he witnessed coming past his home, Flint comments, "The general inclination here, is too much like that of the Tartars. Next to hunting, Indian wars, and the wonderful exuberance of Kentucky, the favourite topic is new countries. They talk of them. They are attached to the associations connected with such conversations. They have a fatal effect upon their exertions. . . . They only make such improvements as they can leave without reluctance and without loss."[16]

John Billingsley, who took part in the migration west of the Mississippi River, in his later years gave an account of his early life in the Arkansas wilderness: "In 1816 we made up about thirty families and lived there two years in all the luxuries of life that a new country could afford, such as buffalo, bear, deer, and elk, and fish and honey; we had pound cake every day, for we beat all the meal we ate in a mortar; and the first year our corn gave out about six weeks before roasting ears came in. Our substitute for bread was venison dried by the fire and then pounded in the mortar and made up in small cakes and fried in bear's oil."[17]

Henry Rowe Schoolcraft, a native of New York who later gained distinction as an ethnologist and Indian agent, traveled through the Ozark region of what is now southern Missouri and northern Arkansas in the late fall and winter of 1818 and 1819. His *Journal of a Tour into the Interior of Missouri and Arkansaw* describes this favored domain of a large number of hunting pioneers. Leaving behind the last outpost of civilization at Potosi, sixty-five miles southwest of

St. Louis, Schoolcraft and his traveling companion, Levi Pettibone, struck off into the wilderness. Three days later they arrived at a major tributary of the Meramec River where several hunting pioneer families lived.[18]

The barking of dogs announced their approach to a hunting pioneer's cabin. The owner was out turkey hunting, but his wife provided them with much information on the surrounding country, including the danger of being robbed or killed by the Osage Indians. "She told us, also, that our guns were not well adapted to our journey; that we should have rifles; and pointed out some other errors in our dress, equipments, and mode of travelling, while we stood in astonishment to hear a woman direct us in matters which we had before thought the peculiar and exclusive province of men. While thus engaged the husband entered, and readily agreed to our proposal, to accompany us toward White River, where he represented the game to exist in great abundance."[19]

Taking three or four large cakes of cornbread and his rifle, the hunter was ready to leave. On their journey, the three men passed villages of Delaware and Shawnee Indians, tribes which recently had migrated westward to this location. The travelers frequently observed deer, bear, and elk. At night they heard the nearby howling of wolves.[20]

Parting company with their hunter guide along the way, Schoolcraft and Pettibone arrived on the north fork of the White River after a journey of three weeks. The men had not seen another person during this entire time. They eventually reached a dwelling and approached it to the accompaniment of loud and continual barking. Several acres were cultivated. A great number of animal skins were in evidence outside the one-room cabin. "Its interior would disappoint any person who has never had an opportunity of witnessing the abode of man beyond the pale of the civilized world. Nothing could be more remote from the ideas we have attached to domestic comfort, neatness, of conveniency, without allusion to cleanliness, order, and the concomitant train of household attributes, which make up the sum of human felicity in refined society." The cabin belonged to a man by the name of Wells, who had a great reputation as a hunter. His sons and daughters wore dirty and greasy deerskin clothing. Hanging from horns on the walls were rifles, shot pouches, leather coats, and dried meat.[21]

The hunting pioneer questioned Schoolcraft and Pettibone about the wild game they had observed on their journey. "He was particularly anxious for bear, deer being very common in all parts, and to use his own words, 'hardly worth shooting;' and from information we gave him, he immediately determined to set out the next day on a bear-hunt, up the Great North Fork. His wife seemed to take a very great interest in this piece of information, and was even more particular than he in inquiries respecting the freshness of the signs we had seen."[22]

Supper was hot cornbread, butter, honey, and milk. Schoolcraft was unsuccessful in his attempt to engage his hostess and her daughters in general small talk. "They could only talk of bears, hunting, and the like. The rude pursuits, and the coarse enjoyments of the hunter state, were all they knew."[23]

Schoolcraft continues, "The evening was now far spent; we had related the most striking incidents of our tour, and had listened in return to many a hunting exploit, in the course of which, the trophies on the wall were occasionally referred to as proof, when a motion was made for sleep, and we lay down on a skin before the fire, happy in the reflection that we had a roof to cover us."[24]

In the morning, Schoolcraft and Pettibone purchased some supplies from their host, who was busy making preparations for the bear hunt with his several sons and a neighbor. For a price, he agreed to guide the travelers a distance of twenty miles and kill a deer for them along the way. The hunting pioneers fulfulled the first part of the agreement, but despite repeated efforts they were unsuccessful in finding a deer. After breakfast the next morning, the hunters suddenly mounted their horses and bid farewell, indifferent to the fact that they were about to leave the travelers deep in the woods with little food for their journey. Schoolcraft and Pettibone were startled and dismayed by this precipitate departure without the terms of their verbal contract having been fulfilled. Watching the backwoodsmen leave, the two men had feelings of disgust mixed with a sense of relief at seeing the last of them. "Nothing could more illy correspond with the ideas we had formed of our reception among white hunters, than the conduct we had experienced from these men. Their avarice, their insensibility to our wants, not to call them sufferings, and their flagrant violations of engagement, has served to sink them in our estimation to a very low standard; for, deprived of its generosity, its open frankness, and hospitality, there is nothing in the hunter-character to admire."[25]

Traveling on through the wilderness, Schoolcraft and Pettibone arrived several days later at the White River near the present-day common border of southwestern Missouri and northwestern Arkansas. There they came upon the log cabin of a "white hunter" named M'Gary. He had several acres of corn under cultivation and some horses, cows, and hogs. "He was provided with a hand-mill for grinding corn, a smoke-house filled with bear and other meats, and the interior of the house, though very far from being either neat or comfortable, bore some evidence that the occupant had once resided in civilized society. I noticed a couple of odd volumes of books upon a shelf. . . . Upon the whole, he appeared to live in great ease and independence, surrounded by a numerous family of sons and daughters, all grown up; received us with cordiality, gave us plenty to eat, and bid us welcome as long as we pleased to stay." The next morning as the travelers were preparing to leave, M'Gary refused to accept any payment for their food and lodging. He then took Schoolcraft to his smokehouse and told him to take what bear or buffalo meat he wanted.[26]

Schoolcraft and Pettibone soon had an opportunity to observe several other hunting pioneer families in this White River area. "These people subsist partly by agriculture, and partly by hunting. . . . Gardens are unknown. Corn and wild meats, chiefly bear's meat, are the staple articles of food. In manners, morals, customs, dress, contempt of labour and hospitality, the state of society is not essentially different from that which exists among the savages." Schoolcraft comments that these backwoods people are strangers to both learning and religion. "Hunting is the principal, the most honourable, and the most profitable employment. To excel in the chace procures fame, and a man's reputation is measured by his skill as a marksman, his agility and strength, his boldness and dexterity in killing game, and his patient endurance and contempt of the hardships of the hunter's life. They are, consequently, a hardy, brave, independent people, rude in appearance, frank and generous, travel without baggage, and can subsist any where in the woods, and would form the most efficient military corps in frontier warfare which can possibly exist." Schoolcraft explains that their way of life inures the hunting pioneers to danger while perfecting them in the use of the rifle. In addition, he believes their normal daily existence is in reality just extended camp service. "Their habitations are not always permanent, having little which is valuable, or loved, to rivet their affections to any one spot; and nothing which is venerated, but what they can carry with them, they frequently change residence, travelling where game is more abundant.

Vast quantities of beaver, otter, raccoon, deer, and bear-skins, are annually caught. These skins are carefully collected and preserved during the summer and fall, and taken down the river in canoes, to the mouth of the Great North Fork of White River, or to the mouth of Black River, where traders regularly come up with large boats to receive them." The hunting pioneers also trade bear and buffalo meat, plus wild honey, for "salt, iron-pots, axes, blankets, knives, rifles, and other articles of first importance in their mode of life."[27]

Schoolcraft points out, "The sabbath is not known by any cessation of the usual avocations of the hunter in this region. To him all days are equally unhallowed, and the first and the last day of the week find him alike sunk in unconcerned sloth, and stupid ignorance." He speculates that the only time these hunting pioneers might acknowledge a dependence on a Supreme Being would be in the midst of a furious storm with lightning and thunder all about them.[28]

"Schools are also unknown, and no species of learning cultivated. Children are wholly ignorant of the knowledge of books, and have not learned even the rudiments of their own tongue. Thus situated, without moral restraint, brought up in the uncontrolled indulgence of every passion and without a regard of religion, the state of society among the rising generation in this region is truly deplorable." Schoolcraft writes that by the time boys are fourteen, they are accomplished in hunting, trapping, and other necessary backwoods skills and ready to support a family. Girls are raised with little care, and they perform much of the daily work. Marriage at an early age is common. In contrast to the observations of many other travelers, Schoolcraft notes that the women seem to bear few children. "This is probably owing wholly to adventitious causes, and may be explained on the same principles as a similar circumstance in savage life, the female being frequently exposed to the inclemency of the weather, always to unusual hardships and fatigues, doing in many instances the man's work, living in camps on the wet ground, without shoes, &c." In addition, many children, deprived of medical aid, die in infancy. One woman told him that it had been several years since she had lived in a cabin with a floor, and the family had moved several times during that period. Four of her children had died before they reached their second year.[29]

Comparing the Indian method of building fires with the process used by the hunting pioneers, Schoolcraft states, "The white hunter, on encamping in his journeys, cuts down green-trees, and builds a large fire of long logs, sitting at some distance from it. The Indian hunts up a few dry limbs, cracks them into little pieces a foot in length, builds a small fire, and sits close by it." Schoolcraft asserts that the Indian gets as much warmth as the hunting pioneer, with only a fiftieth part of the wood and less than half the labor.[30]

Contrasting the habits of the Indian hunter with those of the hunting pioneers, Schoolcraft writes, "The Indian considers the forest his own, and is careful in using and preserving every thing which it affords. He never kills more meat than he has occasion for. The white hunter destroys all before him, and cannot resist the opportunity of killing game, although he neither wants the meat, nor can carry the skins. . . . This is one of the causes of the enmity existing between the white and the red hunters of Missouri."[31]

Schoolcraft says the hunting pioneers, like the Indians, are particularly fond of wild honey. He has observed them gathered around a tree where honey was found, eating prodigious quantities. "When this scene of gluttony was ended, the dog also received his share, as the joint co-partner and sharer of the fatigues, dangers, and enjoyment of the chace; and in no instance have we observed this compact between the dog and the hunter to have been violated. . . ."[32]

According to Schoolcraft, bears in this region retire into caves, rock crevices, or hollow trees during the winter, but they emerge occasionally to forage for food on the mildest days. "Hunters kill this animal during the winter-season by tracking him up to his den, either upon the snow, or by the scent of dogs. If tracked to a large cave, they enter, and often find him in its farthest recess, when he is shot without farther difficulty. If a narrow aperture in the rock, dogs are sent in to provoke him to battle; thus he is either brought in sight within the cave, or driven entirely out of it, and while engaged with the dogs, the hunter walks up deliberately to within a few feet, and pierces him through the heart." If the bear is shot anywhere else but in the heart, it only becomes provoked to the greatest rage. Then several shots may be required to dispatch the animal, as the bear is in continual motion. In the confusion, sometimes dogs are killed either by the bear or accidentally by the hunter. The death of a good hunting dog is considered a serious loss, and the canine's many virtues are extolled long afterward. "When seated around his cabin-fire, the old hunter excites the wonder of his credulous children, gathered into a groupe, to listen to the recital of his youthful deeds, and thus creates in their breasts a desire to follow the same pursuits, and to excel in those hunting exploits which command the universal applause of their companions, and crown with fancied glory the life of the transalleganian hunter, whether red or white."[33]

Schoolcraft reports that beaver also are plentiful in the region. They are highly valued for their fur. "Being web-footed, their favourite region is the water, and they seldom venture far from the banks of the stream they inhabit, and never travel on to the neighbouring highlands." These animals are trapped with a bait concocted of tree bark, herbs, and a "musky substance"; the exact proportions of the ingredients and the method of preparation are kept secret by those skilled in trapping.[34]

Before leaving the wilderness domain of the hunting pioneers, Schoolcraft and Pettibone witnessed a dozen or more of these men in a gathering where the whiskey flowed freely. A wild and riotous night of intoxication ensued within the confines of a small dwelling. "An occasional quarrel gave variety to the scene, and now and then, one drunker than the rest, fell sprawling upon the floor, and for a while remained quiet." Happy to have survived the night, the two sleepless travelers departed at first light, leaving behind some still staggering forms.[35]

Despite the occasional unpleasant encounter on this trip, Schoolcraft was able to highlight the better receptions he and Pettibone had experienced: "Before leaving the banks of White River, it is due to the hardy, frank, and independent hunters, through whose territories we have travelled, and with whom we have from time to time sojourned, to say, that we have been uniformly received at their cabins with a blunt welcome, and experienced the most hospitable and generous treatment. This conduct, which we were not prepared to expect, is the more remarkable in being wholly disinterested, for no remuneration in money for such entertainment (with a very few exceptions,) was ever demanded; but, when presented uniformly refused, on the principle of its not being customary to accept pay of the traveller, for any thing necessary to his sustenance."[36]

Adjacent to Arkansas, the forested wilderness of eastern Oklahoma also was a paradise for the hunting pioneer families. Large numbers of these backwoods people migrated into the region after an 1819 treaty with Spain established that this area was within the boundary of the United States. The frontiersmen built their cabins along the heavily wooded streams where their hogs grew fat on the forest mast. The area abounded in game, including the buffalo. By 1824, it was estimated that two thousand American, French, and Indian hunters were in this region.[37]

From 1840 to 1842, the German traveler Friedrich Gerstacker spent considerable time in Arkansas. Among his writings is an account of a hunting pioneer by the name of John Wells, who lived with his wife and two sons in a well-made log house on a small tributary of the Arkansas River. His neighbors referred to him as "the hunter." Gerstacker notes that this was quite a distinction in an area where everyone hunted and a third of the population did almost nothing else. One cannot help but wonder if this is the same Wells described by Schoolcraft as a great hunter two decades earlier or, perhaps more likely, one of his sons.[38]

Gerstacker describes Wells as bearing some resemblance to the Indians. He had long black hair, and his clothing and moccasins were made of leather which he had tanned himself. He was unexcelled in tracking and stalking game. The wolf found in Wells its most dangerous enemy, and no one was better than he in discovering where a bear was hibernating. Gerstacker comments that Wells, carrying a long rifle and accompanied by his dog, was able to move rapidly and noiselessly through the forest. His eyes took in everything. Lean and agile, he excelled in climbing, jumping, and running. He usually was taciturn and withdrawn; he never spoke loudly, as if fearing to alarm some wild animal.[39]

There was a definite connection between the pioneers in the rugged southern Appalachian Mountains far to the east and those in the gentler Ozark Mountains of southern Missouri and northern Arkansas. These widely separated regions each contained much wild game and included terrain primarily suited to small-scale subsistence agriculture. As a result, portions of both the Appalachians and the Ozarks attracted and then retained many of the hunting pioneers; at the same time, these lands repelled or quickly lost those frontier people seeking optimum farming opportunities. This, of course, was just the opposite of what normally happened in areas more suited to extensive agriculture.

Most of the first pioneers coming to the heavily forested Ozarks were from western Tennessee, western Kentucky, and southern Illinois, regions settled by frontier people who could trace their own or their ancestors' movements from the Appalachians. After a time, however, pioneers began coming directly from the Appalachians, particularly from eastern Tennessee, that early stronghold of pioneer stock. In many cases, this direct migration may have occurred because frontier people in the Ozarks sent word back to friends and relations in the Appalachians informing them that the two areas were very much alike. Sometimes entire family clans migrated, with many Ozark settlements tracing their roots to single counties in the Appalachians. These people were attracted by the rugged terrain which would allow them to continue their way of life, including a major dependence on hunting.[40]

This mode of living continued in remote portions of the Appalachians and Ozarks, as well as in the thickets and wooded swamps of Louisiana and east Texas, much longer than in other areas. In these isolated locations, much of the hunting pioneer lifestyle survived even into the 1900s. Yet, the main dynamic which had characterized life on the forefront of the frontier had disappeared long before. The era in which the true hunting pioneer families moved ever onward into the woodland wilderness effectively had ended in the mid-1800s.

It is to the far south, interestingly, that we must turn for one of the best examples of an individual leading a type of hunting pioneer life long after the vast expanse of woodland wilds east of the Great Plains had ceased to exist. Ben V. Lilly, born in 1856 in Alabama, was too late on the scene to lead the traditional life of a hunting pioneer, but he tried his best. Seeking solitude and wild game, Lilly spent extended periods of time in the remaining wild country of Louisiana and east Texas. Roaming the woods, swamps, and canebrakes where there were few settlers, he was in the domain of bears, panthers, and wild hogs.[41]

Locally renowned for his hunting exploits in the wilderness, Lilly was selected as Theodore Roosevelt's chief huntsman during the president's hunting trip to Tensas Bayou in 1907. In an article entitled "In the Louisiana Canebrakes," published in *Scribner's Magazine*, January 1908, Roosevelt writes, "I never met any other man so indifferent to fatigue and hardship. He equaled Cooper's Deerslayer in woodcraft, in hardihood, in simplicity—and also in loquacity. . . . He could run through the woods like a buck, was far more enduring, and quite as indifferent to weather, though he was over fifty years old." Roosevelt noted that Lilly was as sure as a hound on the track of game, and that he had a great knowledge of wild animals. "He was particularly fond of the chase of the bear, which he followed by himself, with one or two dogs; often he would be on the trail of his quarry for days at a time, lying down to sleep wherever night overtook him; and he had killed over a hundred and twenty bears." Lilly ultimately moved far west to the mountain forests of New Mexico. There he continued roaming the wilds and hunting almost up to the time of his death in 1936, the last tenuous link with the woodland hunting pioneers of an earlier age.[42]

7

SUMMARY

The travel accounts used in this book provide the most valuable and detailed information available on the wilderness people known as the hunting pioneers. From the many eyewitness descriptions, a composite impression may be formed. These frontier families: 1) wanted to live in the wilderness; 2) lived the true backwoods life; 3) prized their freedom and independence; 4) wanted no close neighbors; 5) lived in rough dwellings; 6) hunted frequently, deer and bear being the favored game; 7) caused wanton destruction of wildlife; 8) raised some corn and other patch crops; 9) allowed their horses, cows, and hogs to forage for themselves in the woods; 10) usually had no desire to own land; 11) moved frequently; 12) dressed in animal skin or homemade fabric clothing; 13) spent considerable time at leisure; 14) enjoyed drinking whiskey; 15) engaged in rough-and-tumble fighting; 16) resembled the Native Americans in lifestyle; 17) tended, ironically, to dislike those same Indians; 18) often fought the Indians; 19) viewed the farming pioneers as their ultimate nemeses; and, most importantly, 20) simplified their needs down to the barest essentials.

From this list of characteristics, there emerges a clear picture of the typical hunting pioneer family. Judged by modern values, their most unsettling activities were the willful destruction of wild game, vicious rough-and-tumble fighting, and mutually brutal warfare with the Indians. In contrast, their desire to live freely, independently, and simply in idyllic surroundings, can be appreciated readily today.

More difficult to assess are some of the judgmental terms the travelers used in describing the hunting pioneer families, words which tend to be colored by the observers' own backgrounds. These include: drunken, lazy, heathenish, gloomy, unsociable, licentious, rough, savage, indolent, slovenly, slothful, ferocious, ignorant, insensitive, pleasant, intelligent, honest, kind, calm, dignified, daring, hardy, frank, hospitable, trustworthy, courageous, powerful, and brave. Conflicting views of the hunting pioneers were common; indeed, often they were found within a single writer's account.

There doubtless were some hunting pioneers whose conduct and behavior would have repelled even their peers; others would have fit the most idealized image of a stalwart inhabitant of the deep woods. It seems likely, however, that the majority lived lives somewhere in between. Taking into account the prevailing class biases which many of the travelers could not surmount, one can assume that at least a portion of the hunting pioneer families deserved a more favorable rating than certain of these writers accorded them. Whatever flaws they possessed, the hunting pioneers exhibited great courage and incredible hardiness. These two intrinsically important human attributes, combined with a desire to simplify existence down to the basics, enabled these frontier families to become the ultimate backwoods people. One central fact agreed on by all observers is that the hunting pioneers furnished the dynamic force which pushed the edge of the frontier relentlessly onward through the American woodlands.

In their westward advance, the hunting pioneers were

influenced by powerful forces both behind them and before them. Fleeing from the restraints of a society and civilization which dogged at their heels, these frontier people zealously sought out that ideal wilderness waiting just ahead. In their dedication to a life in the wilds, they were matched among European people only by the voyageurs of interior America and the mountain men of the far West. Unlike many individuals in those two groups, however, the hunting pioneers never planned to return to civilization and brought along their families as evidence of that intention. Moreover, many of the hunting pioneers were born in the backwoods, and those individuals would know no other life. Like the original wilderness dwellers in ages long past, the hunting pioneers considered the wilds to be their only home. Acting as vanguards on the American frontier, they played a critical role in the westward expansion of this nation by inadvertently opening the way for all who followed.

Henry David Thoreau, the patron saint of the modern wilderness movement, wrote at a time when the era of the hunting pioneer had ended. Nevertheless, some of his literary sentiments are uncannily reminiscent of the attitudes of those frontiersmen. In an 1851 lecture, Thoreau spoke "for Nature, for absolute freedom and wildness." It was in this same forum that he stated the now famous phrase "in Wildness is the preservation of the World."[1]

Although Thoreau had visited real wilderness in Maine, he never immersed himself in such wilds permanently as did the hunting pioneers. It is in *Walden,* which details his experiences in the relatively tame sylvan haunts near his home in Concord, Massachusetts, that Thoreau wrote many of his most-quoted statements relating to wilderness. In a declaration which any hunting pioneer would understand, Thoreau writes, "I went to the woods because I wished to live deliberately, to front only the essential facts of life, and see if I could not learn what it had to teach, and not, when I came to die, discover that I had not lived. . . . . I wanted to live deep and suck out all the marrow of life, to live so sturdily and Spartan-like as to put to rout all that was not life, to cut a broad swath and shave close, to drive life into a corner, and reduce it to its lowest terms, and, if it proved to be mean, why then to get the whole and genuine meanness of it, and publish its meanness to the world; or if it were sublime, to know it by experience, and be able to give a true account of it in my next excursion."[2]

Thoreau pities the young men in his area "whose misfortune it is to have inherited farms" with all their attendant chores of tilling, mowing, and raising cattle, work which crushes and smothers them under the burden. Thoreau's attitude toward agricultural labor exhibits the same bias against the farming life shown by the hunting pioneers. This view, in part, led Thoreau to his famous statement: "The mass of men lead lives of quiet desperation."[3]

Elaborating on the virtues of the simple life, Thoreau avows, "I would rather sit on a pumpkin and have it all to myself, than be crowded on a velvet cushion." He goes on to say that the very simplicity of man's existence in primitive times made him a "sojourner in nature." Refreshed with food and sleep, he traveled on through valleys, plains, and mountains. "We now no longer camp for a night, but have settled down on earth and forgotten heaven." Later, in words which seem to reverberate from the days of the hunting pioneers, Thoreau asserts, "Our life is frittered away by detail. . . . Simplicity, simplicity, simplicity! I say, let your affairs be as two or three, and not a hundred or a thousand; instead of a million count half a dozen, and keep your accounts on your thumbnail. . . . Simplify, Simplify."[4]

John Muir, another giant figure in modern wilderness

thought, is most famous for his years of extensive rambles in the Sierras of California. However, in 1867, before migrating to the West, he made a tour through what once had been the domain of the hunting pioneers. Crossing the Ohio River from Indiana into central Kentucky, Muir moved eastward into the still relatively unscathed mountains. He marveled at the grandeur of the scenery which revealed to him the hand of the Creator. In his book, *A Thousand-Mile Walk to the Gulf*, Muir describes the view from a mountaintop. Like Filson's colorful and descriptive quote attributed to Daniel Boone during his time as a long hunter, the comments are heartfelt: "The scenery is far grander than any I ever before beheld. The view extends from the Cumberland Mountains on the north far into Georgia and North Carolina to the south, an area of about five thousand square miles. Such an ocean of wooded, waving, swelling mountain beauty and grandeur is not to be described. Countless forest-clad hills, side by side in rows and groups, seemed to be enjoying the rich sunshine and remaining motionless only because they were so eagerly absorbing it. All were united by curves and slopes of inimitable softness and beauty."[5]

The physical wilderness has been altered greatly since the days of the hunting pioneers and since Thoreau's and Muir's era as well. The current wilderness movement is driven by the dual objectives of saving the remnants of wild land which still exist and allowing other areas to become wild again. The goal is to protect the wilderness scene for posterity in parks, forests, and other natural areas. There, people can still catch a glimpse of what it was that set the hunting pioneers' hearts ablaze. These denizens of the backcountry forged a singular bond with the wilderness which was truly extraordinary. This unique and all-encompassing relationship with the forest frontier is the hunting pioneers' final legacy, echoing from the deep woods.

NOTES

CHAPTER 1

[1] Terry G. Jordan and Matti Kaups, *The American Backwoods Frontier: An Ethnic and Ecological Interpretation* (Baltimore: The Johns Hopkins University Press, 1989), p. 36.

[2] Johann David Schoepf, *Travels in the Confederation, 1783-1784*, ed. and trans. Alfred J. Morrison (Philadelphia: William J. Campbell, 1911), pp. 238-239.

[3] Michael Williams, *Americans and their Forests: A Historical Geography* (Cambridge: Cambridge University Press, 1989), pp. 3-4, 32-49.

[4] Elias Pym Fordham, *Personal Narrative of Travels in Virginia, Maryland, Pennsylvania, Ohio, Indiana, Kentucky; and of a Residence in the Illinois Territory: 1817-1818*, ed. Frederick Austin Ogg (Cleveland: Arthur H. Clark Company, 1906), p. 178.

[5] Ibid.

[6] Richard A. Bartlett, *The New Country: A Social History of the American Frontier, 1776-1890* (New York: Oxford University Press, 1974), pp. 12-16.

[7] Roderick Nash, *Wilderness and the American Mind* (New Haven: Yale University Press, 1982), pp. 23-28.

[8] Ray Allen Billington, *Frederick Jackson Turner: Historian, Scholar, Teacher* (New York: Oxford University Press, 1973), p. 451; Gregory H.

Nobles, *American Frontiers: Cultural Encounters and Continental Conquest* (New York: Hill and Wang, 1997), pp. 8-14; Allan G. Bogue, *Frederick Jackson Turner: Strange Roads Going Down* (Norman: University of Oklahoma Press, 1998), p. 53; Frederick Jackson Turner, *The Frontier in American History* (New York: Holt, Rinehart and Winston, 1962), pp. 2-4, 12.

[9] Dale Van Every, *Forth to the Wilderness: The First American Frontier 1754-1774* (New York: William Morrow and Company, 1961), pp. 38-44.

[10] C. A. Weslager, *The Delaware Indians: A History* (New Brunswick, N.J.: Rutgers University Press, 1972), pp. 56-62.

[11] Nash, pp. 29-30.

[12] Karen Ordahl Kupperman, *Settling With the Indians: The Meeting of English and Indian Cultures in America, 1580-1640* (Totowa, N.J.: Rowman and Littlefield, 1980), pp. 80-106; Roy Harvey Pearce, *Savagism and Civilization: A Study of the Indian and the American Mind* (Baltimore: The Johns Hopkins Press, 1953), pp. 66-75; Bernard W. Sheehan, *Savagism and Civility: Indians and Englishmen in Colonial Virginia* (Cambridge: Cambridge University Press, 1980), pp. ix-x, 1-3.

[13] Stephen Aron, *How the West Was Lost: The Transformation of Kentucky from Daniel Boone to Henry Clay* (Baltimore: The Johns Hopkins University Press, 1996), pp. 13-15.

[14] Robert W. McCluggage, "The Pioneer Squatter," *Illinois Historical Journal* 82, no. 1 (Spring 1989), p. 51.

[15] J. Hector St. John de Crevecoeur, *Letters from an American Farmer* (London: J. M. Dent and Sons Ltd., 1912), pp. 46-47.

[16] Benjamin Rush, *Letters of Benjamin Rush*, ed. L. H. Butterfield, vol. 1 (Princeton: Princeton University Press, 1951), p. 400.

[17] Ibid., pp. 400-401.

[18] Ibid., p. 401.

[19] Joe Kindig, Jr., *Thoughts on the Kentucky Rifle in Its Golden Age* (York, Penn.: George Shumway Publisher, 1960), pp. 1-2, 25-26.

[20] Kindig, pp. 4, 25-30; John G. W. Dillin, *The Kentucky Rifle* (York, Penn.: Greorge Shumway Publisher, 1975), p. 121; Henry J. Kauffman, *The Pennsylvania-Kentucky Rifle* (Harrisburg, Penn.: The Stackpole Company, 1960), p. 19.

[21] Kindig., pp. 2-3, 26, 30-32.

[22] G. M. Trevelyan, *English Social History: A Survey of Six Centuries Chaucer to Queen Victoria* (London: Longmans, Green and Company Ltd., 1944), p. 279; Matt Cartmill, *A View to a Death in the Morning: Hunting and Nature through History* (Cambridge: Harvard University Press, 1993), pp. 60-67.

[23] Arthur K. Moore, *The Frontier Mind: A Cultural Analysis of the Kentucky Frontiersman* (Lexington: University of Kentucky Press, 1957), p. 200.

[24] Jordan and Kaups, pp. 119-123.

[25] James Flint, *Letters from America, 1818-1820,* in *Early Western Travels, 1748-1846,* ed. Reuben Gold Thwaites, vol. 9 (Cleveland: Arthur H. Clark Company, 1904), pp. 232-233.

[26] Turner, pp. 19-20.

[27] Turner, p. 20.

[28] Ray Allen Billington, *Westward Expansion: A History of the American Frontier* (New York: Macmillan Publishing Company, Inc., 1974), p. 5.

[29] Annette Kolodny, *The Land Before Her: Fantasy and Experience of the American Frontiers, 1630-1860* (Chapel Hill: The University of North Carolina Press, 1984), pp. 5-13.

CHAPTER 2

[1] Max Oelschlaeger, *The Idea of Wilderness: From Prehistory to the Age of Ecology* (New Haven: Yale University Press, 1991), pp. 9-14; William H. McNeill, *The Rise of the West: A History of the Human Community* (Chicago: The University of Chicago Press, 1963), pp. 11-18.

[2] Nash, pp. 8-20; George H. Williams, *Wilderness and Paradise in Christian Thought: The Biblical Experience of the Desert in the History of Christianity and the Paradise Theme in the Theological Idea of the University* (New York: Harper and Brothers, 1962), pp. 10-18, 22-23; Clarence J. Glacken, *Traces on the Rhodian Shore: Nature and Culture in Western Thought from Ancient Times to the End of the Eighteenth Century* (Berkeley: University of California Press, 1967), pp. 320-321; Cartmill, pp. 56-60.

[3] Nash, pp. 23-29.

[4] Jordan and Kaups, pp. 3-4, 53-63, 211-232; C. A. Weslager, *The Log Cabin in America* (New Brunswick, N.J.: Rutgers University Press, 1969), pp. 141, 150-152, 201-202.

[5] Jordan and Kaups, pp. 36-37.

[6] Wayland Fuller Dunaway, *The Scotch-Irish of Colonial Pennsylvania* (Chapel Hill: The University of North Carolina Press, 1944), pp. 13-20; James G. Leyburn, *The Scotch-Irish: A Social History* (Chapel Hill: The University of North Carolina Press, 1962), pp. 3-13; T. C. Smout, *A History of the Scottish People 1560-1830* (New York: Charles Scribner's Sons, 1969), pp. 19-71.

[7] Leyburn, pp. 108-132.

[8] Dunaway, pp. 28-33; David Hackett Fischer, *Albion's Seed: Four British Folkways in America* (New York: Oxford University Press, 1989), pp. 605-621; Jordan and Kaups, pp. 61-62.

[9] Dunaway, pp. 181-182; Grady McWhiney, *Cracker Culture: Celtic Ways*

in the Old South (Tuscaloosa: The University of Alabama Press, 1988), pp. xxi-xliii, 1-22, 51-79.

[10] Leyburn, pp. 191-199; Dunaway, p. 182.

[11] Leyburn, pp. 199-200; William Beidelman, *The Story of the Pennsylvania Germans: Embracing an account of their Origin, their History, and their Dialect* (Detroit: Gale Research Company, 1969), pp. 22-34.

[12] Van Every, pp. 301-304; Leyburn, pp. 199-210.

[13] Van Every, p. 304; William Byrd, *The Prose Works of William Byrd of Westover: Narratives of a Colonial Virginian,* ed. Louis B. Wright (Cambridge: Harvard University Press, 1966), p. 312.

[14] William J. Hinke and Charles E. Kemper, eds., "Moravian Diaries of Travels Through Virginia," *The Virginia Magazine of History and Biography* 11, no. 2 (October 1903), p. 122.

[15] Ibid., p. 123.

[16] John Bakeless, *Daniel Boone* (Harrisburg, Penn.: Stackpole Company, 1965), pp. 8-18; Lyman C. Draper, *The Life of Daniel Boone,* ed. Ted Franklin Belue (Mechanicsburg, Penn.: Stackpole Books, 1998), pp. 101-125; John Mack Faragher, *Daniel Boone: The Life and Legend of an American Pioneer* (New York: Henry Holt and Company, 1992), pp. 9-29; Reuben Gold Thwaites, *Daniel Boone* (New York: Chelsea House, 1983), pp. 9-17.

[17] Bakeless, pp. 18-20; Draper, pp. 126-128; Faragher, pp. 29-33; Thwaites, pp. 17-18.

[18] Hayes Baker-Crothers, *Virginia and the French and Indian War* (Chicago: The University of Chicago Press, 1928), pp. 82-105; William A. Hunter, *Forts on the Pennsylvania Frontier, 1753-1758* (Harrisburg: The Pennsylvania Historical and Museum Commission, 1960), pp. 168-193, 214-217, 301-305, 365-372, 548-564; Francis Jennings, *Empire of Fortune: Crown, Colonies, and Tribes in the Seven Years War in America* (New

York: W. W. Norlon and Company, 1998), pp. 187-196; Douglas Edward Leach, *Arms for Empire: A Military History of the British Colonies in North America, 1607-1763* (New York: The Macmillan Company, 1973), pp. 378-379, 389-391.

[19] Bakeless, pp. 20-32; Draper, pp. 128-169; Faragher, pp. 36-53; Thwaites, pp. 21-50; David H. Corkran, *The Cherokee Frontier: Conflict and Survival, 1740-62* (Norman: University of Oklahoma Press, 1962), pp. 163-254; Tom Hatley, *The Dividing Paths: Cherokees and South Carolinians Through the Era of the Revolution* (New York: Oxford University Press, 1993) pp. 105-154.

[20] Charles Woodmason, *The Carolina Backcountry on the Eve of the Revolution: The Journal and Other Writings of Charles Woodmason, Anglican Itinerant*, ed. Richard J. Hooker (Chapel Hill: The University of North Carolina Press, 1953), p. 25.

[21] Ibid., p. 39.

[22] Ibid., p. 52.

[23] Ibid., p. 61.

[24] Rachel N. Klein, *Unification of a Slave State: The Rise of the Planter Class in the South Carolina Backcountry, 1760-1808* (Chapel Hill: The University of North Carolina Press, 1990), pp. 51-56.

[25] Ibid., pp. 56-64.

[26] Crevecoeur, pp. 51-52.

[27] Ibid., pp. 52-53.

[28] Ibid., p. 53.

[29] Ibid., pp. 54-55.

[30] Bakeless, pp. 32-43; Draper, pp. 169-203; Faragher, pp. 53-67; Thwaites, pp. 56-70.

[31] Samuel Cole Williams, *Dawn of Tennessee Valley and Tennessee History* (Johnson City, Tenn.: The Watauga Press, 1937), pp. 334-354.

[32] Ibid., p. 358.

[33] Mark A. Baker, *Sons of a Trackless Forest: The Cumberland Long Hunters of the Eighteenth Century* (Franklin, Tenn.: Baker's Trace Publishing, 1997), pp. 21, 89-90; Ted Franklin Belue, *The Long Hunt: Death of the Buffalo East of the Mississippi* (Mechanicsburg, Penn.: Stackpole Books, 1996), p. 86.

[34] Baker, pp. 115-142; Belue, pp. 86-88.

[35] Harriette Simpson Arnow, *Seedtime on the Cumberland* (New York: The Macmillan Company, 1960), p. 155; Baker, pp. 777-819; Belue, p. 86.

[36] Arnow, pp. 148, 152; Baker, pp. 103-106, 373-374; Belue, pp. 89-90.

[37] Baker, pp. 207-222; Belue, pp. 88-89.

[38] Arnow, pp. 153-154; Baker, pp. 217, 343-345; Belue, pp. 81-84.

[39] Arnow, p. 165.

[40] Bakeless, pp. 44-65; Draper, pp. 204-280, 238-247; Faragher, pp. 68-87; Thwaites, pp. 71-96.

[41] John Filson, *The Discovery, Settlement and present State of Kentucke* (Gloucester, Mass.: Peter Smith, 1975), pp. 54-56; Bakeless, pp. 394-395; Faragher, pp. 6-7; Thwaites, pp. 199-200.

[42] Bakeless, pp. 66-74; Draper, pp. 283-290; Faragher, pp. 89-95; Thwaites, pp. 101-103.

[43] Michael N. McConnell, *A Country Between: The Upper Ohio Valley and Its Peoples, 1724-1774* (Lincoln: University of Nebraska Press, 1992), pp. 167-168; Albert T. Volwiler, *George Croghan and the Westward Movement 1741-1782* (Cleveland: The Arthur H. Clark Company, 1926),

pp. 210-211.

[44] Jennings, pp. 438-451; Francis Parkman, *The Conspiracy of Pontiac and the Indian War after the Conquest of Canada* (Boston: Little, Brown, and Company, 1933), 1:179-198, 2:3-60, 88-114; Howard H. Peckham, *Pontiac and the Indian Uprising* (Princeton, N.J.: Princeton University Press, 1947), pp. 92-111, 154-170, 214-220; Van Every, pp. 123-124, 194-205.

[45] James Axtell, *The Invasion Within: The Contest of Cultures in Colonial North America* (New York: Oxford University Press, 1985), pp. 302-327; Jennings, pp. 196-199.

[46] J. Norman Heard, *White Into Red: A Study of the Assimilation of White Persons Captured by Indians* (Metuchen, N.J.: The Scarecrow Press, Inc., 1973), pp. 9-10.

[47] Parkman, 2:253-254.

[48] Van Every, pp. 255-263.

[49] McConnell, pp. 244-258.

[50] Volwiler, p. 211; K. G. Davies, ed., *Documents of the American Revolution, 1770-1783* (Dublin: Irish University Press Ltd., 1974), 5:203.

[51] Richard White, *The Middle Ground: Indians, Empires, and Republics in the Great Lakes Region, 1650-1815* (Cambridge: Cambridge University Press, 1991), p. 341.

[52] Davies, 8:253, 258.

[53] Van Every, pp. 257-261.

CHAPTER 3

[1] John E. Ferling, *A Wilderness of Miseries: War and Warriors in Early America* (Westport, Conn.: Greenwood Press, 1980), pp. 32-33; Francis Jennings, *The Invasion of America: Indians, Colonialism, and the Cant of*

Conquest (Chapel Hill: The University of North Carolina Press, 1975), pp. 59-61; Sheehan, pp. ix-x, 1-5, 37-38, 56, 63; J. Leitch Wright, Jr., *The Only Land They Knew: The Tragic Story of the American Indians in the Old South* (New York: The Free Press, 1981), pp. 7-10.

[2] James Axtell, *Beyond 1492: Encounters in Colonial North America* (New York: Oxford University Press, 1992), pp. 37-58, 104-105; Jennings, *The Invasion of America*, p. 32; Kupperman, pp. 80-86; Sheehan, pp. 5-6.

[3] Ferling, pp. 32, 40; Verner W. Crane, *The Southern Frontier 1670-1732* (Durham, N.C.: Duke University Press, 1929), pp. 17-21; Jennings, *The Invasion of America*, pp. 22-31; Wright, pp. 22-26; Axtell, *Beyond 1492*, pp. 105-106.

[4] Leroy V. Eid, "'A Kind of Running Fight': Indian Battlefield Tactics in the Late Eighteenth Century," *The Western Pennsylvania Historical Magazine* 71, no. 2 (April 1988), pp. 149-150; Ferling, pp. 35-37; Jennings, *The Invasion of America*, pp. 149-155; Armstrong Starkey, *European and Native American Warfare, 1675-1815* (Norman: University of Oklahoma Press, 1998), pp. 25-26; Sheehan, pp. 5-8, 37, 63.

[5] Ferling, pp. 34-35, 47-50; Jennings, *The Invasion of America*, p. 160; Starkey, pp. 26-27, 30-31.

[6] Nathaniel Knowles, "The Torture of Captives by the Indians of Eastern North America," *Proceedings of the American Philosophical Society* 82, no. 2 (March 1940), pp. 151-152, 156-173, 180-193, 202-203, 208-209; Ferling, pp. 50-54; Jennings, *The Invasion of America*, pp. 160-163.

[7] Gregory Evans Dowd, *A Spirited Resistance: The North American Indian Struggle for Unity, 1745-1815* (Baltimore: The Johns Hopkins University Press, 1992), pp. xiii-xv.

[8] Kupperman, pp. 101-102; Starkey, pp. 20-22, 71-82.

[9] Byrd, p. 219.

[10] Eid, pp. 147-152; Starkey, p. 18.

[11] Eid, pp. 152-154; Starkey, pp. 21-22, 127, 131.

[12] Eid, pp. 152-159; John K. Mahon, "Anglo-American Methods of Indian Warfare, 1676-1794," *The Mississippi Valley Historical Review* 45, no. 2 (September 1958), pp. 260-261; Starkey, p. 22.

[13] Elizabeth A. Perkins, *Border Life: Experience and Memory in the Revolutionary Ohio Valley* (Chapel Hill: The University of North Carolina Press, 1998), p. 132.

[14] Albert H. Tillson, *Gentry and Common Folk: Political Culture on a Virginia Frontier 1740-1789* (Lexington: The University Press of Kentucky, 1991), pp. 47, 51-55.

[15] Robert Rogers, *Journals of Major Robert Rogers* (Ann Arbor, Mich.: University Microfilms, Inc., 1966), pp. 60-70.

[16] McConnell, pp. 255-279; Bakeless, pp. 77-80; Draper, pp. 307-310; Faragher, pp. 100-102; Thwaites, pp. 106-107.

[17] Otis K. Rice, *The Allegheny Frontier: West Virginia Beginnings, 1730-1830* (Lexington: The University Press of Kentucky, 1970), pp. 82-83; Reuben Gold Thwaites and Louise Phelps Kellogg, eds., *Documentary History of Dunmore's War 1774* (Madison: Wisconsin Historical Society, 1905), pp. 151-156; Van Every, pp. 334-335.

[18] Tillson, pp. 47-58.

[19] Ibid., pp. 51-53.

[20] Virgil A. Lewis, *History of the Battle of Point Pleasant* (Charleston, W.Va.: The Tribune Printing Company, 1909), pp. 30-39; Rice, pp. 83-85; Van Every, pp. 335-341.

[21] Lewis, pp. 41-48; Rice, p. 85; Thwaites and Kellogg, pp. 254-259; Van Every, pp. 341-343.

[22] Lewis, pp. 44-48; Rice, p. 85; Thwaites and Kellogg, pp. 264, 271-274, 286-287; Van Every, p. 343; Mahon, pp. 271-272.

[23] Lewis, pp. 45-52; Rice, pp. 85-87; Thwaites and Kellogg, pp. 256, 259, 264-265, 274-276, 287-288; Van Every, pp. 343-344.

[24] Bakeless, pp. 81-82; Draper, pp. 310-313; Faragher, pp. 102-106; Thwaites, pp. 108-112.

[25] Colin G. Calloway, *The American Revolution in Indian Country: Crisis and Diversity in Native American Communities* (Cambridge: Cambridge University Press, 1995), pp. 1-25.

[26] Calloway, pp. 26-32; Starkey, p. 113.

[27] Calloway, pp. 31-32; Starkey, pp. 113-119.

[28] White, pp. 367, 378.

[29] Rachel N. Klein, "Frontier Planters and the American Revolution: The South Carolina Backcountry, 1775-1782," in *An Uncivil War: The Southern Backcountry during the American Revolution*, ed. Ronald Hoffman, et. al. (Charlottesville: The University Press of Virginia, 1985), pp. 37-69.

[30] Eric Hinderaker, *Elusive Empires: Constructing Colonialism in the Ohio Valley, 1673-1800* (Cambridge: Cambridge University Press, 1997), p. 214.

[31] Perkins, pp. 62-65.

[32] Ibid., pp. 63-71.

[33] Bakeless, pp. 89-140; Draper, pp. 329-434; Faragher, pp. 112-140; Thwaites, pp. 113-136.

[34] John P. Brown, *Old Frontiers: The Story of the Cherokee Indians from Earliest Times to the Date of Their Removal to the West, 1838* (Kingsport, Tenn.: Southern Publishers, Inc., 1938), pp. 148-151; John Haywood, *The Civil and Political History of the State of Tennessee from its Earliest Settlements up to the Year 1796* (Knoxville: Tenase Company, 1969), pp. 62-63; J. G. M. Ramsey, *The Annals of Tennessee to the End of the Eighteenth Century* (Charleston: Walker and James, 1853), p. 154; Grace

Steele Woodward, *The Cherokees* (Norman: University of Oklahoma Press, 1963), pp. 88-95.

[35] Brown, p. 151; Haywood, pp. 63-64; Ramsey, pp. 154-155; Woodward, pp. 95-96.

[36] Bakeless, p. 148; Draper, pp. 435-437; Faragher, p. 153; Thwaites, pp. 142-143.

[37] Bakeless, pp. 195-213; Draper, pp. 500-508; Faragher, pp. 182-192; Thwaites, pp. 160-162.

[38] Bakeless, pp. 212-225; Draper, pp. 509-518; Faragher, pp. 192-198; Thwaites, pp. 162-164.

[39] Draper, pp. 518-519; Faragher, p. 198.

[40] Bakeless, *Background to Glory: The Life of George Rogers Clark* (Lincoln: University of Nebraska Press, 1992), pp. 45-55; William Hayden English, *Conquest of the Country Northwest of the River Ohio 1778-1783 and Life of Gen. George Rogers Clark* (Indianapolis: The Bowen-Merrill Company, 1896), 1:84-85, 466-468; James Alton James, *The Life of George Rogers Clark* (New York: Greenwood Press, Publishers, 1969), pp. 69, 112.

[41] Bakeless, *Background to Glory*, pp. 55-56; English, 1:87-94, 124-129, 468-473; James, pp. 112-116.

[42] Bakeless, *Background to Glory*, pp. 61-106; English, 1:131-214, 473-510; James, pp. 117-130.

[43] Bakeless, *Background to Glory*, pp. 121-139; English, 1:215-242; James, pp. 131-135.

[44] Bakeless, *Background to Glory*, pp. 149-178; English, 1:265-316, 518-532; James, pp. 136-143.

[45] Bakeless, *Background to Glory*, pp. 179-187; English, 1:317-328, 532-533, 585-586; James, p. 143.

[46] Bakeless, *Background to Glory*, pp. 187-196; English, 1:328-335, 533-536; James, p. 143.

[47] Bakeless, *Background to Glory*, pp. 196-199; English, 1:335-343, 536-540; James, pp. 143-144.

[48] Bakeless, *Background to Glory*, pp. 199-210; English, 1:343-350, 541; James, pp. 144-145.

[49] Bakeless, *Background to Glory*, pp. 232-233; English, 1:358-369, 545-546, 552-553; James, pp. 151, 170-171.

[50] John Bradford, *The Voice of the Frontier: John Bradford's Notes on Kentucky*, ed. Thomas D. Clark (Lexington: The University Press of Kentucky, 1993), pp. 26-27; Emilius O. Randall, *History of Ohio: The Rise and Progress of an American State* (New York: The Century History Company, 1912), 2:269-273; Charles Gano Talbert, *Benjamin Logan: Kentucky Frontiersman* (Lexington: University of Kentucky Press, 1962), pp. 74-81.

[51] Bakeless, *Background to Glory*, pp. 258-259; English, 2:680-681; Faragher, pp. 209-210; James, pp. 210-211; Talbert, p. 108.

[52] Bakeless, *Background to Glory*, pp. 260-263; Bradford, p. 39; English, 2:681-682; James, p. 211; Talbert, pp. 108-113.

[53] Bakeless, *Background to Glory*, pp. 263-266; Bradford, pp. 40-41; English, 2:682; James, pp. 211-213; Talbert, p. 113.

[54] Bakeless, *Background to Glory*, pp. 266-268; Bradford, pp. 41-42; English, 2:682-683; James, p. 213; Talbert, p. 114.

[55] Lyman C. Draper, *King's Mountain and Its Heroes: History of the Battle of King's Mountain, October 7th, 1780, and the Events Which Led to It* (New York: Dauber and Pine Bookshops, Inc., 1929), pp. 68-122; Haywood, pp. 77-80; Dale Van Every, *A Company of Heroes: The American Frontier 1775-1783*, (New York: William Morrow and Company, 1962), pp. 227-229.

[56] Draper, *King's Mountain and Its Heroes*, pp. 165-197; Haywood, pp. 80-81; Van Every, *A Company of Heroes*, pp. 229-230.

[57] Draper, *King's Mountain and Its Heroes*, pp. 197-235; Haywood, pp. 81-83; Van Every, *A Company of Heroes*, pp. 230-231.

[58] Draper, *King's Mountain and Its Heroes*, pp. 236-238, 243-250.

[59] Draper, *King's Mountain and Its Heroes*, pp. 250-263; Van Every, *A Company of Heroes*, pp. 231-232.

[60] Draper, *King's Mountain and Its Heroes*, pp. 297-306, 330-343; Van Every, *A Company of Heroes*, p. 232.

[61] Consul W. Butterfield, *An Historical Account of the Expedition against Sandusky under Col. William Crawford in 1782* (Cincinnati: Robert Clarke and Company, 1873), pp. 33-61; Andrew R. L. Cayton, *The Frontier Republic: Ideology and Politics in the Ohio Country, 1780-1825* (Kent, Ohio: The Kent State University Press, 1986), p. 3; R. Douglas Hurt, *The Ohio Frontier: Crucible of the Old Northwest, 1720-1830* (Bloomington: Indiana University Press, 1996), pp. 144-145; Randall, pp. 317-338.

[62] Butterfield, pp. 62-80, 136-181; Randall, pp. 347-354.

[63] Butterfield, pp. 202-219; Randall, pp. 354-359.

[64] Butterfield, pp. 219-251; Randall, pp. 359-361.

[65] Butterfield, pp. 311-361.

[66] Bakeless, *Daniel Boone*, pp. 271-291; Faragher, pp. 215-217; Thwaites, pp. 185-188.

[67] Bakeless, *Daniel Boone*, pp. 291-297; Faragher, pp. 217-219; Thwaites, pp. 188-189.

[68] Bakeless, *Daniel Boone*, pp. 297-303; Faragher, pp. 219-222; Thwaites, pp. 189-190.

[69] Bakeless, *Background to Glory*, pp. 293-300; English, 2:758-760; James, pp. 276-278; Talbert, pp. 171-181.

[70] Bakeless, *Background to Glory*, pp. 319-324; English, 2:795-803; James, pp. 347-356.

[71] Bakeless, *Daniel Boone*, pp. 316-318; Faragher, pp. 251-255; Talbert, pp. 209-212.

CHAPTER 4

[1] Bakeless, *Daniel Boone*, pp. 324-336; Faragher, pp. 235-242; Thwaites, pp. 192-198, 200-202.

[2] Bakeless, *Daniel Boone*, pp. 340-350; Faragher, pp. 242-249, 260-263; Thwaites, pp. 208-210.

[3] Bakeless, *Daniel Boone*, pp. 394-395; Faragher, pp. 2-7; Thwaites, pp. 199-200; Richard Slotkin, *Regeneration Through Violence: The Mythology of the American Frontier, 1600-1860* (Middletown, Conn.: Wesleyan University Press, 1973), pp. 313-316.

[4] Jean-Jacques Rousseau, *The First and Second Discourses together with the Replies to Critics and Essay on the Origin of Languages*, ed. and trans. Victor Gourevitch (New York: Harper and Row, Publishers, 1986), p. 177.

[5] Francis Baily, *Journal of a Tour in Unsettled Parts of North America in 1796 and 1797*, ed. Jack D. L. Holmes (Carbondale: Southern Illinois University Press, 1969), pp. 70-71.

[6] Ibid., pp. 71-72.

[7] Ibid., pp. 115-116.

[8] Ibid., p. 116.

[9] Georges Henri Victor Collot, *A Journey in North America* (New York: AMS Press, 1974), 1:109-110.

[10] Ibid., 1:110-112.

[11] Ibid., 1:128, 172-173.

[12] Ibid., 1:185-187.

[13] Francois Andre Michaux, *Travels to the West of the Alleghany Mountains in the States of Ohio, Kentucky, and Tennessee,* in *Early Western Travels, 1748-1846,* ed. Reuben Gold Thwaties, vol. 3 (Cleveland: Arthur H. Clark Company, 1904), pp. 189-191.

[14] Ibid., p. 192.

[15] Ibid., pp. 192-193.

[16] Ibid., p. 193.

[17] Thaddeus Mason Harris, *Journal of a Tour into the Territory Northwest of the Allegheny Mountains: Made in the Spring of the Year 1803,* in *Early Western Travels, 1748-1846,* ed. Reuben Gold Thwaites, vol. 3 (Cleveland: Arthur H. Clark Company, 1904), p. 358.

[18] Fortescue Cuming, *Sketches of a Tour to the Western Country, through the States of Ohio and Kentucky,* in *Early Western Travels, 1748-1846,* ed. Reuben Gold Thwaites, vol. 4 (Cleveland: Arthur H. Clark Company, 1904), p. 137.

[19] Ibid., pp. 134, 137.

[20] Ibid., pp. 153-154.

[21] Ibid., p. 137.

[22] Elliot J. Gorn, "'Gouge and Bite, Pull Hair and Scratch': The Social Significance of Fighting in the Southern Backcountry," *The American Historical Review* 90, no. 1 (February 1985), pp. 18-43.

[23] Michael Allen, *Western Rivermen, 1763-1861: Ohio and Mississippi*

Boatmen and the Myth of the Alligator Horse (Baton Rouge: Louisiana State University Press, 1990), pp. 90-94.

[24] Cuming, pp. 176-177.

[25] Ibid., pp. 177-178.

[26] Cayton, pp. 1-11; Randolph Chandler Downes, *Frontier Ohio, 1788-1803* (Columbus: The Ohio State Archeological and Historical Society, 1935), pp. 73-74; Hurt, pp. 143-148.

[27] Cayton, pp. 1-2; Walter Havighurst, *Wilderness for Sale: The Story of the First Western Land Rush* (New York: Hastings House, Publishers, 1956), pp. 68-71, 108-110.

[28] Hurt, pp. 179-186, 249-253; Dale Van Every, *Ark of Empire: The American Frontier 1784-1803* (New York: William Morrow and Company, 1963), pp. 196-200.

[29] Hurt, pp. 249-262.

[30] John Stillman Wright, *Letters From the West; or A Caution to Emigrants* (Ann Arbor, Mich.: University Microfilms, Inc., 1966), pp. 21-22.

[31] John D. Barnhart and Dorothy L. Riker, *Indiana to 1816: The Colonial Period* (Indianapolis: Indiana Historical Bureau and Indiana Historical Society, 1971), p. 318; R. Carlyle Buley, *The Old Northwest: Pioneer Period 1815-1840* (Indianapolis: Indiana Historical Society, 1950), 1:26.

[32] Fordham, pp. 96, 187-188.

[33] William Faux, *Memorable Days in America: Being a Journal of a Tour to the United States*, in *Early Western Travels, 1748-1846*, ed. Reuben Gold Thwaites, vol. 11 (Cleveland: Arthur H. Clark Company, 1905), pp. 203-204.

[34] Hugh McCulloch, *Men and Measures of a Half Century*, in *Travel Accounts of Indiana 1679-1961*, comp. Shirley S. McCord (Indianapolis: Indiana Historical Bureau, 1970), pp. 144-145.

CHAPTER 5

[1] Arrell M. Gibson, *The Kickapoos: Lords of the Middle Border* (Norman: University of Oklahoma Press, 1963), pp. 13-15; R. David Edmunds, *The Potawatomis: Keepers of the Fire* (Norman: University of Oklahoma Press, 1978), pp. 48-49, 91, 96; William T. Hagan, *The Sac and Fox Indians* (Norman: University of Oklahoma Press, 1958), pp. 4-5.

[2] Gibson, pp. 47-48, 54-57; Edmunds, pp. 153-158.

[3] James E. Davis, *Frontier Illinois* (Bloomington: Indiana University Press, 1998), pp. 135-139, 143-151; Gibson, pp. 70-71; Edmunds, pp. 193-194; Hagan, pp. 60-72.

[4] James A. Clifton, *The Prairie People: Continuity and Change in Potawatomi Indian Culture 1665-1965* (Lawrence: The Regents Press of Kansas, 1977), pp. 216-217; Edmunds, p. 215; Gibson, p. 78; Hagan, pp. 83-85.

[5] Gershom Flagg, "Pioneer Letter," in *The Prairie State: A Documentary History of Illinois, Colonial Years to 1860*, ed. Robert P. Sutton (Grand Rapids, Mich.: William B. Eerdmans Publishing Company, 1976), p. 143.

[6] Ibid.

[7] Ibid., p. 142.

[8] Henry Bradshaw Fearon, *Sketches of America: A Narrative of a Journey of Five Thousand Miles Through the Eastern and Western States of America* (London: Longman, Hurst, Rees, Orme, and Brown, 1818), p. 261.

[9] Wright, p. 34.

[10] Morris Birkbeck, *Notes on a Journey from the Coast of Virginia to the Territory of Illinois*, in *Pictures of Illinois One Hundred Years Ago*, ed. Milo Milton Quaife (Chicago: R. R. Donnelly and Sons Company, 1918), p. 5.

[11] Ibid.

[12] Ibid., p. 6.

[13] Ibid., pp. 6-7.

[14] Ibid., pp. 7-10.

[15] Ibid., pp. 8-9.

[16] Ibid., p. 10.

[17] Ibid., pp. 11-12.

[18] Ibid., pp. 12-13.

[19] Ibid., pp. 31-32.

[20] Ibid., pp. 33-34.

[21] Ibid., p. 34.

[22] George Flower, *History of the English Settlement in Edwards County Illinois, Founded in 1817 and 1818, by Morris Birkbeck and George Flower,* in *Chicago Historical Society's Collection,* vol. 1 (Chicago: Fergus Printing Company, 1882), p. 66.

[23] Ibid., pp. 66-67.

[24] Ibid., pp. 67-68.

[25] Ibid., p. 68.

[26] Ibid., pp. 68-69.

[27] Ibid., pp. 69-70.

[28] Ibid., pp. 71-72.

[29] Ibid., p. 72.

[30] Ibid., p. 184.

[31] Fordham, p. 119.

[32] Ibid., pp. 125-126.

[33] Ibid., pp. 126-127.

[34] Ibid., pp. 127-128, 145, 224.

[35] Ibid., pp. 181-182.

[36] Ibid., pp. 224-225.

[37] Faux, p. 237.

[38] Ibid., pp. 259-260, 303-304.

[39] William Newnham Blane, *An Excursion Through the United States and Canada During the Years 1822-23*, in *Pictures of Illinois One Hundred Years Ago*, ed. Milo Milton Quaife (Chicago: R. R. Donnelly Sons Company, 1918), pp. 49-50.

[40] Ibid., pp. 63-65.

[41] Ibid., pp. 68-69.

[42] Ibid., p. 66.

[43] Ibid., pp. 66-67.

[44] Ibid., p. 67.

[45] William Vipond Pooley, "The Settlement of Illinois From 1830 to 1850," *Bulletin of the University of Wisconsin* 220, vol. 1, no. 4 (May 1908), p. 324.

[46] John Mack Faragher, *Sugar Creek: Life on the Illinois Prairie* (New Haven: Yale University Press, 1986), pp. 3-17, 39-52.

[47] Gibson, pp. 78-86.

[48] Lois A. Carrier, *Illinois: Crossroads of a Continent* (Urbana: University of Illinois Press, 1993), pp. 56-58.

[49] Pooley, p. 327.

[50] A. D. Jones, *Illinois and the West* (Boston: Weeks, Jordan and Company, 1838), pp. 88-93.

[51] Pooley, pp. 328-329.

[52] Cecil Eby, *"That Disgraceful Affair,"* The Black Hawk War (New York: W. W. Norton and Company, Inc., 1973), p. 82.

[53] Hagan, pp. 141-191; Roger L. Nichols, *Black Hawk and the Warrior's Path* (Arlington Heights, Ill.: Harlan Davidson, Inc., 1992), pp. 101-135.

[54] Pooley, pp. 382-384, 538-539.

[55] Eliza W. Farnham, *Life in Prairie Land* (Urbana: University of Illinois Press, 1988), pp. 265-267.

[56] Ibid., p. 267.

[57] Ibid., pp. 267-268.

[58] William Oliver, *Eight Months in Illinois* (Ann Arbor, Mich.: University Microfilms, Inc., 1966), pp. 81-82.

[59] Ibid., p. 82.

[60] Ibid., p. 83.

[61] Ibid., pp. 83-84.

[62] Ibid., p. 86.

[63] Ibid., p. 80.

[64] Ibid., pp. 80-81.

[65] Ibid., p. 81.

CHAPTER 6

[1] Everett Dick, *The Dixie Frontier: A Social History of the Southern Frontier from the First Transmontane Beginnings to the Civil War* (New York: Capricorn Books, 1948), pp. 23-29, 32-36.

[2] Paul Russell Cutright, *Theodore Roosevelt: The Making of a Conservationist* (Urbana: University of Illinois Press, 1985), pp. 172-173.

[3] Davy Crockett, *Davy Crockett's Own Story as written by Himself: The Autobiography of America's Great Folk Hero* (Stamford, Conn.: Longmeadow Press, 1992), p. 55.

[4] James Atkins Shackford, *David Crockett: The Man and the Legend* (Chapel Hill: The University of North Carolina Press, 1956), pp. 62-63, 77.

[5] Crockett, pp. 112, 123-124.

[6] John James Audubon, *Delineations of American Scenery and Character* (New York: G. A. Baker and Company, 1926), pp. 41-42.

[7] Ibid., pp. 42-43.

[8] Ibid., p. 43.

[9] Ibid., pp. 43-46.

[10] Ibid., pp. 68-75.

[11] Bakeless, *Daniel Boone*, pp. 355-360; Faragher, *Daniel Boone*, pp. 274-276; Thwaites, pp. 220-222.

[12] Bakeless, *Daniel Boone*, pp. 371-383; Faragher, *Daniel Boone*, pp. 277-281, 291-294, 307-308; Thwaites, pp. 223-228.

[13] Bakeless, *Daniel Boone*, p. 371; Faragher, *Daniel Boone*, pp. 313-314.

[14] Bakeless, *Daniel Boone*, pp. 384-387; Faragher, *Daniel Boone*, pp. 281-285.

[15] Thwaites, pp. 228-229; Bakeless, *Daniel Boone*, pp. 391-392.

[16] Timothy Flint, *Recollections of the Last Ten Years, Passed in Occasional Residences and Journeyings in the Valley of the Mississippi* (Boston: Cummings, Hilliard, and Company, 1826), pp. 204-205.

[17] C. Fred Williams, et. al., eds., *A Documentary History of Arkansas* (Fayetteville: The University of Arkansas Press, 1984), p. 18.

[18] Henry Rowe Schoolcraft, *Rude Pursuits and Rugged Peaks: Schoolcraft's Ozark Journal 1818-1819*, ed. Milton D. Rafferty (Fayetteville: The University of Arkansas Press, 1996), pp. 19-23.

[19] Ibid., p. 23.

[20] Ibid., pp. 23-24, 26.

[21] Ibid., pp. 52-53.

[22] Ibid., p. 54.

[23] Ibid., pp. 54-55.

[24] Ibid., p. 55.

[25] Ibid., pp. 55-57.

[26] Ibid., pp. 59-61.

[27] Ibid., pp. 62-64.

[28] Ibid., p. 73.

[29] Ibid., p. 74.

[30] Ibid., pp. 78-79.

[31] Ibid., p. 79.

[32] Ibid., p. 86.

[33] Ibid., pp. 88-89.

[34] Ibid., pp. 89-90.

[35] Ibid., pp. 108-109.

[36] Ibid., p. 113.

[37] Grant Foreman, *Indians and Pioneers: The Story of the American Southwest Before 1830* (Norman: University of Oklahoma Press, 1936), pp. 139-142.

[38] Friedrich Gerstacker, *In the Arkansas Backwoods: Tales and Sketches*, ed. and trans. James William Miller (Columbia: University of Missouri Press, 1991), pp. 96-97.

[39] Ibid., pp. 97-99.

[40] Ellen Gray Massey, *Bittersweet Country* (Garden City, N.Y.: Anchor Press/Doubleday, 1978), pp. 2-6.

[41] J. Frank Dobie, *The Ben Lilly Legend* (Austin: University of Texas Press, 1994), pp. 21-27.

[42] Ibid., pp. 98-100.

SUMMARY

[1] Nash, p. 84.

[2] Henry David Thoreau, *Walden*, ed. Walter Harding (Boston: Houghton Mifflin Company, 1995), p. 87.

[3] Ibid., pp. 3, 6.

[4] Ibid., pp. 34-35, 88.

[5] John Muir, *A Thousand-Mile Walk to the Gulf* (Dunwoody, Ga.: Norman S. Berg, Publisher, n. d.), pp. 30, 38-39.

BIBLIOGRAPHY

PRIMARY SOURCES

Audubon, John James. *Delineations of American Scenery and Character*. New York: G. A. Baker and Company, 1926.

Baily, Francis. *Journal of a Tour in Unsettled Parts of North America in 1796 and 1797*. Edited by Jack D. L. Holmes. Carbondale: Southern Illinois University Press, 1969.

Birkbeck, Morris. *Notes on a Journey from the Coast of Virginia to the Territory of Illinois*. In *Pictures of Illinois One Hundred Years Ago*, edited by Milo Milton Quaife. Chicago: R. R. Donnelley and Sons Company, 1918.

Blane, William Newnham. *An Excursion Through the United States and Canada During the Years 1822-23*. In *Pictures of Illinois One Hundred Years Ago*, edited by Milo Milton Quaife. Chicago: R. R. Donnelley and Sons Company, 1918.

Bradford, John. *The Voice of the Frontier: John Bradford's Notes on Kentucky*. Edited by Thomas D. Clark. Lexington: The University Press of Kentucky, 1993.

Byrd, William. *The Prose Works of William Byrd of Westover: Narratives of a Colonial Virginian*. Edited by Louis B. Wright. Cambridge: Harvard University Press, 1966.

Collot, Georges Henri Victor. *A Journey in North America*, vol. 1. New York: AMS Press, 1974.

Crevecoeur, J. Hector St. John de. *Letters from an American Farmer*. London: J. M. Dent and Sons Ltd., 1912.

Crockett, Davy. *Davy Crockett's Own Story as written by Himself: The Autobiography of America's Great Folk Hero*. Stamford, Conn.: Longmeadow Press, 1992.

Cuming, Fortescue. *Sketches of a Tour to the Western Country, through the States of Ohio and Kentucky*. In *Early Western Travels, 1748-1846*, edited by Reuben Gold Thwaites, vol. 4. Cleveland: The Arthur H. Clark Company, 1904.

Davies, K. G., ed. *Documents of the American Revolution 1770-1783*, vols. 5 and 8. Dublin: Irish University Press Ltd., 1974.

Farnham, Eliza W. *Life in Prairie Land*. Urbana: University of Illinois Press, 1988.

Faux, William. *Memorable Days in America: Being a Journal of a Tour to the United States*. In *Early Western*

Travels, 1748-1846, edited by Reuben Gold Thwaites, vol. ll. Cleveland: Arthur H. Clark Company, 1905.

Fearon, Henry Bradshaw. *Sketches of America: A Narrative of a Journey of Five Thousand Miles Through the Eastern and Western States of America.* London: Longman, Hurst, Rees, Orme, and Brown, 1818.

Filson, John. *The Discovery, Settlement and present State of Kentucke.* Gloucester, Mass.: Peter Smith, 1975.

Flagg, Gershom. "Pioneer Letter." In *The Prairie State: A Documentary History of Illinois, Colonial Years to 1860,* edited by Robert P. Sutton. Grand Rapids, Mich.: William B. Eerdmans Publishing Company, 1976.

Flint, James. *Letters from America, 1818-1820.* In *Early Western Travels, 1748-1846,* edited by Reuben Gold Thwaites, vol. 9. Cleveland: Arthur H. Clark Company, 1904.

Flint, Timothy. *Recollections of the Last Ten Years, Passed in Occasional Residences and Journeyings in the Valley of the Mississippi.* Boston: Cummings, Hilliard, and Company, 1826.

Flower, George. *History of the English Settlement in Edwards County Illinois, Founded in 1817 and 1818, by Morris Birkbeck and George Flower.* In *Chicago Historical Society's Collection,* vol. 1. Chicago: Fergus Printing Company, 1882.

Fordham, Elias Pym. *Personal Narrative of Travels in*

Virginia, Maryland, Pennsylvania, Ohio, Indiana, Kentucky; and of a Residence in the Illinois Territory: 1817-1818. Edited by Frederick Austin Ogg. Cleveland: Arthur H. Clark Company, 1906.

Gerstacker, Friedrich. *In the Arkansas Backwoods: Tales and Sketches.* Edited and translated by James William Miller. Columbia: University of Missouri Press, 1991.

Harris, Thaddeus Mason. *Journal of a Tour into the Territory Northwest of the Alleghany Mountains: Made in the Spring of the Year 1803.* In *Early Western Travels, 1748-1846,* edited by Reuben Gold Thwaites, vol. 3. Cleveland: Arthur H. Clark Company, 1904.

Hinke, William J. and Charles E. Kemper, eds. "Moravian Diaries of Travels Through Virginia." *The Virginia Magazine of History and Biography* 11, no. 2 (October 1903): 113-131.

Jones, A. D. *Illinois and the West.* Boston: Weeks, Jordan and Company, 1838.

McCulloch, Hugh. *Men and Measures of a Half Century.* In *Travel Accounts of Indiana 1679-1961,* compiled by Shirley S. McCord. Indianapolis: Indiana Historical Bureau, 1970.

Michaux, Francois Andre. *Travel to the West of the Alleghany Mountains in the States of Ohio, Kentucky, and Tennessee.* In *Early Western Travels, 1748-1846,* edited by Reuben Gold Thwaites, vol. 3. Cleveland: Arthur H. Clark Company, 1904.

Muir, John. *A Thousand-Mile Walk to the Gulf.* Dunwoody, Ga.: Norman S. Berg, Publisher, n.d.

Oliver, William. *Eight Months in Illinois.* Ann Arbor, Mich.: University Microfilms, Inc., 1966.

Rogers, Robert. *Journals of Major Robert Rogers.* Ann Arbor, Mich.: University Microfilms, Inc., 1966.

Rousseau, Jean-Jacques. *The First and Second Discourses together with the Replies to Critics and Essay on the Origin of Languages.* Edited and translated by Victor Gourevitch. New York: Harper and Row, Publishers, 1986.

Rush, Benjamin. *Letters of Benjamin Rush,* vol. 1. Edited by L. H. Butterfield. Princeton: Princeton University Press, 1951.

Schoepf, Johann David. *Travels in the Confederation, 1783-1784.* Edited and translated by Alfred J. Morrison. Philadelphia: William J. Campbell, 1911.

Schoolcraft, Henry Rowe. *Rude Pursuits and Rugged Peaks: Schoolcraft's Ozark Journal 1818-1819.* Edited by Milton D. Rafferty. Fayetteville: The University of Arkansas Press, 1996.

Thoreau, Henry David. *Walden.* Edited by Walter Harding. Boston: Houghton Mifflin Company, 1995.

Thwaites, Reuben Gold and Louise Phelps Kellogg, eds.

Documentary History of Dunmore's War 1774. Madison: Wisconsin Historical Society, 1905.

Williams, C. Fred et. al., eds. *A Documentary History of Arkansas.* Fayetteville: The University of Arkansas Press, 1984.

Woodmason, Charles. *The Carolina Backcountry on the Eve of the Revolution: The Journal and Other Writings of Charles Woodmason, Anglican Itinerant.* Edited by Richard J. Hooker. Chapel Hill: The University of North Carolina Press, 1953.

Wright, John Stillman. *Letters From the West; or A Caution to Emigrants.* Ann Arbor, Mich.: University Microfilms, Inc., 1966.

SECONDARY SOURCES

Allen, Michael. *Western Rivermen, 1763-1861: Ohio and Mississippi Boatmen and the Myth of the Alligator Horse.* Baton Rouge: Louisiana State University Press, 1990.

Arnow, Harriette Simpson. *Seedtime on the Cumberland.* New York: The Macmillan Company, 1960.

Aron, Stephen. *How the West Was Lost: The Transformation of Kentucky from Daniel Boone to Henry Clay.* Baltimore: The Johns Hopkins University Press, 1996.

Axtell, James. *Beyond 1492: Encounters in Colonial North America*. New York: Oxford University Press, 1992.

—————. *The Invasion Within: The Contest of Cultures in Colonial North America*. New York: Oxford University Press, 1985.

Bakeless, John. *Background to Glory: The Life of George Rogers Clark*. Lincoln: University of Nebraska Press, 1992.

—————. *Daniel Boone*. Harrisburg, Penn.: Stackpole Company, 1965.

Baker, Mark A. *Sons of a Trackless Forest: The Cumberland Long Hunters of the Eighteenth Century*. Franklin, Tenn.: Baker's Trace Publishing, 1998.

Baker-Crothers, Hayes. *Virginia and the French and Indian War*. Chicago: The University of Chicago Press, 1928.

Barnhart, John D. and Dorothy L. Riker. *Indiana to 1816: The Colonial Period*. Indianapolis: Indiana Historical Bureau and Indiana Historical Society, 1971.

Bartlett, Richard A. *The New Country: A Social History of the American Frontier, 1776-1890*. New York: Oxford University Press, 1974.

Beidelman, William. *The Story of the Pennsylvania Germans: Embracing an account of their Origin, their History, and their Dialect*. Detroit: Gale Research Company, 1969.

Belue, Ted Franklin. *The Long Hunt: Death of the Buffalo East of the Mississippi.* Mechanicsburg, Penn.: Stackpole Books, 1996.

Billington, Ray Allen. *Frederick Jackson Turner: Historian, Scholar, Teacher.* New York: Oxford University Press, 1973.

————. *Westward Expansion: A History of the American Frontier.* New York: Macmillan Publishing Company, Inc., 1974.

Bogue, Allan G. *Frederick Jackson Turner: Strange Roads Going Down.* Norman: University of Oklahoma Press, 1998.

Brown, John P. *Old Frontiers: The Story of the Cherokee Indians from Earliest Times to the Date of Their Removal to the West, 1838.* Kingsport, Tenn.: Southern Publishers, Inc., 1938.

Buley, R. Carlyle. *The Old Northwest: Pioneer Period 1815-1840,* vol. 1. Indianapolis: Indiana Historical Society, 1950.

Butterfield, Consul W. *An Historical Account of the Expedition against Sandusky under Col. William Crawford in 1782.* Cincinnati: Robert Clarke and Company, 1873.

Calloway, Colin G. *The American Revolution in Indian Country: Crisis and Diversity in Native American Communities.* Cambridge: Cambridge University Press,

1995.

Carrier, Lois A. *Illinois: Crossroads of a Continent*. Urbana: University of Illinois Press, 1993.

Cartmill, Matt. *A View to a Death in the Morning: Hunting and Nature through History*. Cambridge: Harvard University Press, 1993.

Cayton, Andrew R. L. *The Frontier Republic: Ideology and Politics in the Ohio Country, 1780-1825*. Kent, Ohio: The Kent State University Press, 1986.

Clifton, James A. *The Prairie People: Continuity and Change in Potawatomi Indian Culture 1665-1965*. Lawrence: The Regents Press of Kansas, 1977.

Corkran, David H. *The Cherokee Frontier: Conflict and Survival, 1740-62*. Norman: University of Oklahoma Press, 1962.

Crane, Verner W. *The Southern Frontier 1670-1732*. Durham, N.C.: Duke University Press, 1928.

Cutright, Paul Russell. *Theodore Roosevelt: The Making of a Conservationist*. Urbana: University of Illinois Press, 1985.

Davis, James E. *Frontier Illinois*. Bloomington: Indiana University Press, 1998.

Dick, Everett. *The Dixie Frontier: A Social History of the Southern Frontier from the First Transmontane*

Beginnings to the Civil War. New York: Capricorn Books, 1948.

Dillin, John G. W. *The Kentucky Rifle*. York, Penn.: George Shumway Publisher, 1975.

Dobie, J. Frank. *The Ben Lilly Legend*. Austin: University of Texas Press, 1994.

Dowd, Gregory Evans. *A Spirited Resistance: The North American Indian Struggle for Unity, 1745-1815*. Baltimore: The Johns Hopkins University Press, 1992.

Downes, Randolph Chandler. *Frontier Ohio, 1788-1803*. Columbus: The Ohio State Archeological and Historical Society, 1935.

Draper, Lyman C. *King's Mountain and Its Heroes: History of the Battle of King's Mountain, October 7th, 1780, and the Events Which Led To It*. New York: Dauber and Pine Bookshops, Inc., 1929.

————. *The Life of Daniel Boone*. Edited by Ted Franklin Belue. Mechanicsburg, Penn.: Stackpole Books, 1998.

Dunaway, Wayland Fuller. *The Scotch-Irish of Colonial Pennsylvania*. Chapel Hill: The University of North Carolina Press, 1944.

Eby, Cecil. *"That Disgraceful Affair," the Black Hawk War*. New York: W. W. Norton and Company, Inc., 1973.

Edmunds, R. David. *The Potawatomis: Keepers of the Fire.*

Norman: University of Oklahoma Press, 1978.

Eid, Leroy V. "'A Kind of Running Fight': Indian Battlefield Tactics in the Late Eighteenth Century." *The Western Pennsylvania Historical Magazine* 71, no. 2 (April 1988): 147-171.

English, William Hayden. *Conquest of the Country Northwest of the River Ohio 1778-1783 and Life of Gen. George Rogers Clark*, 2 vols. Indianapolis: The Bowen-Merrill Company, 1896.

Faragher, John Mack. *Daniel Boone: The Life and Legend of an American Pioneer*. New York: Henry Holt and Company, 1992.

————. *Sugar Creek: Life on the Illinois Prairie*. New Haven: Yale University Press, 1986.

Ferling, John E. *A Wilderness of Miseries: War and Warriors in Early America*. Westport, Conn.: Greenwood Press, 1980.

Fischer, David Hackett. *Albion's Seed: Four British Folkways in America*. New York: Oxford University Press, 1989.

Foreman, Grant. *Indians and Pioneers: The Story of the American Southwest Before 1830*. Norman: University of Oklahoma Press, 1936.

Gibson, Arrel M. *The Kickapoos: Lords of the Middle Border*. Norman: University of Oklahoma Press, 1963.

Glacken, Clarence J. *Traces on the Rhodian Shore: Nature and Culture in Western Thought from Ancient Times to the End of the Eighteenth Century*. Berkeley: University of California Press, 1967.

Gorn, Elliott J. "'Gouge and Bite, Pull Hair and Scratch': The Social Significance of Fighting in the Southern Backcountry." *The American Historical Review* 90, no. 1 (February 1985): 18-43.

Hagan, William T. *The Sac and Fox Indians*. Norman: University of Oklahoma Press, 1958.

Hatley, Tom. *The Dividing Paths: Cherokees and South Carolinians Through the Era of Revolution*. New York: Oxford University Press, 1993.

Havighurst, Walter. *Wilderness for Sale: The Story of the First Land Rush*. New York: Hastings House, Publishers, 1956.

Haywood, John. *The Civil and Political History of the State of Tennessee from its Earliest Settlement up to the Year 1796*. Knoxville: Tenase Company, 1969.

Heard, J. Norman. *White Into Red: A Study of the Assimilation of White Persons Captured by Indians*. Metuchen, N.J.: The Scarecrow Press, Inc., 1973.

Hinderaker, Eric. *Elusive Empires: Constructing Colonialism in the Ohio Valley, 1673-1800*. Cambridge: Cambridge University Press, 1997.

Hunter, William A. *Forts on the Pennsylvania Frontier, 1753-1758.* Harrisburg: The Pennsylvania Historical and Museum Commission, 1960.

Hurt, R. Douglas. *The Ohio Frontier: Crucible of the Old Northwest, 1720-1830.* Bloomington: Indiana University Press, 1996.

James, James Alton. *The Life of George Rogers Clark.* New York: Greenwood Press, Publishers, 1969.

Jennings, Francis. *Empire of Fortune: Crown, Colonies, and Tribes in the Seven Years War in America.* New York: W. W. Norton and Company, 1988.

————. *The Invasion of America: Indians, Colonialism, and the Cant of Conquest.* Chapel Hill: The University of North Carolina Press, 1975.

Jordan, Terry G. and Matti Kaups. *The American Backwoods Frontier: An Ethnic and Ecological Interpretation.* Baltimore: The Johns Hopkins University Press, 1989.

Kauffman, Henry J. *The Pennsylvania-Kentucky Rifle.* Harrisburg, Penn.: The Stackpole Company, 1960.

Kindig, Joe Jr. *Thoughts on the Kentucky Rifle in Its Golden Age.* York, Penn.: George Shumway Publishers, 1960.

Klein, Rachel N. "Frontier Planters and the American Revolution: The South Carolina Backcountry, 1775-1782." In *An Uncivil War: The Southern Backcountry during the American Revolution,* edited by Ronald

Hoffman, et. al. Charlottesville: The University Press of Virginia, 1985.

————. *Unification of a Slave State: The Rise of the Planter Class in the South Carolina Backcountry, 1760-1808.* Chapel Hill: The University of North Carolina Press, 1990.

Knowles, Nathaniel. "The Torture of Captives by the Indians of Eastern North America." *Proceedings of the American Philosophical Society* 82, no. 2 (March 1940): 151-225.

Kolodny, Annette. *The Land Before Her: Fantasy and Experience of the American Frontiers, 1630-1860.* Chapel Hill: The University of North Carolina Press, 1984.

Kupperman, Karen Ordahl. *Settling With the Indians: The Meeting of English and Indian Cultures in America, 1580-1640.* Totowa, N.J.: Rowman and Littlefield, 1980.

Leach, Douglas Edward. *Arms for Empire: A Military History of the British Colonies in North America, 1607-1763.* New York: The Macmillan Company, 1973.

Lewis, Virgil A. *History of the Battle of Point Pleasant.* Charleston, W.Va.: The Tribune Printing Company, 1909.

Leyburn, James G. *The Scotch-Irish: A Social History.* Chapel Hill: The University of North Carolina Press, 1962.

Mahon, John K. "Anglo-American Methods of Indian Warfare, 1676-1794." *The Mississippi Valley Historical Review* 45, no. 2 (September 1958): 254-275.

Massey, Ellen Gray. *Bittersweet Country*. Garden City, N.Y.: Anchor Press/Doubleday, 1978.

McCluggage, Robert W. "The Pioneer Squatter." *Illinois Historical Journal* 82, no. 1 (Spring 1989): 47-54.

McConnell, Michael N. *A Country Between: The Upper Ohio Valley and Its Peoples, 1724-1774*. Lincoln: University of Nebraska Press, 1992.

McNeill, William H. *The Rise of the West: A History of the Human Community*. Chicago: The University of Chicago Press, 1963.

McWhiney, Grady. *Cracker Culture: Celtic Ways in the Old South*. Tuscaloosa: The University of Alabama Press, 1988.

Moore, Arthur K. *The Frontier Mind: A Cultural Analysis of the Kentucky Frontiersman*. Lexington: The University of Kentucky Press, 1957.

Nash, Roderick. *Wilderness and the American Mind*. New Haven: Yale University Press, 1982.

Nichols, Roger L. *Black Hawk and the Warrior's Path*. Arlington Heights, Ill.: Harlan Davidson, Inc., 1992.

Nobles, Gregory H. *American Frontiers: Cultural Encounters and Continental Conquest.* New York: Hill and Wang, 1997.

Oelschlaeger, Max. *The Idea of Wilderness: From Prehistory to the Age of Ecology.* New Haven: Yale University Press, 1991.

Parkman, Francis. *The Conspiracy of Pontiac and the Indian War after the Conquest of Canada,* 2 vols. Boston: Little, Brown, and Company, 1933.

Pearce, Roy Harvey. *Savagism and Civilization: A Study of the Indian and the American Mind.* Baltimore: The Johns Hopkins Press, 1953.

Peckham, Howard H. *Pontiac and the Indian Uprising.* Princeton, N.J.: Princeton University Press, 1947.

Perkins, Elizabeth A. *Border Life: Experience and Memory in the Revolutionary Ohio Valley.* Chapel Hill: The University of North Carolina Press, 1998.

Pooley, William Vipond. "The Settlement of Illinois From 1830 to 1850." *Bulletin of the University of Wisconsin* 220, vol. 1, no. 4 (May 1908): 287-595.

Ramsey, J. G. M. *The Annals of Tennessee to the End of the Eighteenth Century.* Charleston: Walker and James, 1853.

Randall, Emilius O. *History of Ohio: The Rise and Progress of an American State,* vol. 2. New York: The Century

History Company, 1912.

Rice, Otis K. *The Allegheny Frontier: West Virginia Beginnings, 1730-1830.* Lexington: The University Press of Kentucky, 1970.

Shackford, James Atkins. *David Crockett: The Man and the Legend.* Chapel Hill: The University of North Carolina Press, 1956.

Sheehan, Bernard W. *Savagism and Civility: Indians and Englishmen in Colonial Virginia.* Cambridge: Cambridge University Press, 1980.

Slotkin, Richard. *Regeneration Through Violence: The Mythology of the American Frontier, 1600-1860.* Middletown, Conn.: Wesleyan University Press, 1973.

Smout, T. C. *A History of the Scottish People 1560-1830.* New York: Charles Scribner's Sons, 1969.

Starkey, Armstrong. *European and Native American Warfare, 1675-1815.* Norman: University of Oklahoma Press, 1998.

Talbert, Charles Gano. *Benjamin Logan: Kentucky Frontiersman.* Lexington: The University of Kentucky Press, 1962.

Thwaites, Reuben Gold. *Daniel Boone.* New York: Chelsea House, 1983.

Tillson, Albert H. *Gentry and Common Folk: Political Culture on a Virginia Frontier 1740-1789.* Lexington: The University Press of Kentucky, 1991.

Trevelyan, G. M. *English Social History: A Survey of Six Centuries Chaucer to Queen Victoria.* London: Longmans, Green and Company, 1944.

Turner, Frederick Jackson. *The Frontier in American History.* New York: Holt, Rinehart and Winston, 1962.

Van Every, Dale. *A Company of Heroes: The American Frontier 1775-1783.* New York: William Morrow and Company, 1962.

―――――. *Ark of Empire: The American Frontier 1784-1803.* New York: William Morrow and Company, 1963.

―――――. *Forth to the Wilderness: The First American Frontier 1754-1774.* New York: William Morrow and Company, 1961.

Volwiler, Albert T. *George Croghan and the Westward Movement 1741-1782.* Cleveland: The Arthur H. Clark Company, 1926.

Weslager, C. A. *The Delaware Indians: A History.* New Brunswick, N.J.: Rutgers University Press, 1972.

―――――. *The Log Cabin in America: From Pioneer Days to the Present.* New Brunswick, N.J.: Rutgers University Press, 1969.

White, Richard. *The Middle Ground: Indians, Empires, and*

Republics in the Great Lakes Region, 1650-1815. Cambridge: Cambridge University Press, 1991.

Williams, George H. *Wilderness and Paradise in Christian Thought: The Biblical Experience of the Desert in the History of Christianity and The Paradise Theme in the Theological Idea of the University.* New York: Harper and Brothers, 1962.

Williams, Michael. *Americans and their Forests: A Historical Geography.* Cambridge: Cambridge University Press, 1989.

Williams, Samuel Cole. *Dawn of Tennessee Valley and Tennessee History.* Johnson City, Tenn.: The Watauga Press, 1937.

Woodward, Grace Steele. *The Cherokees.* Norman: University of Oklahoma Press, 1963.

Wright, J. Leitch, Jr. *The Only Land They Knew: The Tragic Story of the American Indians in the Old South.* New York: The Free Press, 1981.

INDEX